Written by: Dana Rose Glore-Gray
Copyright: 2011

Published by: D' Rose Institute of Urevia &
Subtle Energies Healing Center
www.reiki-ureviaclasses.com or
www.urevia.com

Urevia

The Journey is The Teacher

TABLE OF CONTENTS

Introduction

This book is written from two points of view. The first is from a character named Seeker who is a student. Seeker's adventures are documented in the parable journal entries. These entries describe Seeker's spiritual experiences, thoughts, feelings, and relationship with the Divine. The Parable journal entries are written to be a realistic representation of what it's like for a beginner to communicate with angels and spirit guides, so therefore; they are beautifully simple.

The second point of view is written from a teacher, facilitator, or guide's perspective and is found in the chapter sections of this book, where wisdom is offered to facilitate Seeker's healing process and enlightenment.

This format allows the reader to see what it might be like to take a similar journey in his or hers own life, as well as offer valuable, practical wisdom that can be immediately applied in everyday relationships and experiences.

This book is for anyone considering spiritual exploration and growth through healing, wisdom, and love.

"THE JOURNEY IS THE TEACHER."

Parable One
Journal Entry
"Doubt"

"Too good to be true," I'm thinking as I look at the group of people in my Reiki healing class that I signed up for on a whim. I'm supposed to channel healing energy after some kind of attunement process, and magically help heal someone by laying my hands on him or her. This guy, the teacher, is telling me it will assist in the healing of any pain or stress by balancing the energy field that flows

around and through us, known as the aura. Sitting in this healing class, I am feeling doubtful. The teacher is so sure, so open, and so getting on my nerves! Everything's wonderful; everyone's special. Well, I'm not feeling that special. As a matter of fact, I feel little if anything at all. He's going on about some warm sensation I'm supposed to be feeling in the palms of my hands when the healing energy flows through me.

Well, before I go any further with my mental tirade of personal indecision, I should introduce myself: Seeker is my name, and doubt is my game. I am looking for a connection; to myself, to others, and to God. I am seeking an understanding of my world and my place in it. I decided to continue my quest by experiencing something new, like a healing class.

I'm lying on the massage table fully clothed, 'thank God,' and I am feeling a little uncomfortable. Okay, a lot uncomfortable, while four people are practicing the hand positions used during a healing session on me. I'm feeling a slight warming sensation. I'm supposed to feel something or see something more, right? Where's my spiritual experience? Where are my buzzy feelings, my white doves, my heart opening and being filled with God's splendor? The only things I can think of are, "Oops, I ate too much for lunch and this gal's hands are pressing too hard on my stomach," and "Back off, would ya?" Of course, outwardly I say nothing. Just nod and do what the teacher tells me to do.

I'm trying to remind myself that this is all new and I need to give myself the time to digest the new information, but I'm not naturally a patient person. I prefer to know where I'm going instead of waiting for it to unfold.

Later, towards the end of the day, while I'm driving home, I wonder how this new information about healing energy is going to fit into my daily life. I also wonder if it's even real or some guru's imagination and a bunch of people who needed spiritual comfort, jumped on the bandwagon.

I want to believe in an invisible healing energy that I'm somehow worthy of channeling, but my religious upbringing and lack of knowledge create doubt. Even if this spiritually guided, universal-energy mumbo jumbo is real, does it take me away from my religious beliefs or does it bring me closer to my relationship with Goddess/God within and without?

Oh hell, I don't know. I know I feel drawn to experience my spirituality in a physical way. As I'm driving home, I decide to check it out a little more. This time, my experiences will decide my beliefs, rather than someone else's interpretation of what is and isn't real.

Returning home and pulling into my driveway, I am peaceful. I will not let myself be taken in without *having a genuine sense of it, but I'm not being overly guarded either. Before I discount the new idea of Metaphysical universal energy, I will think about it. I will wait, process, and see where this **"choice"** leads me.*

Chapter One

More than a belief, it's an experience.

We don't *believe* we are alive; we *know* it. How do we *know* it? We *feel* it. Just like we cannot see the wind, but we know it's there because we can feel it caress our skin. God, angels, and healing energies are similar. When a person experiences a healing session, he or she feels the nurturing effects of the energy filling the body and aura. It is difficult to explain and simply needs to be experienced. Healings or energy medicine transcends rationality and speaks to the heart. A person will know immediately if healings can offer a positive contribution to his or her journey. It exceeds expectations, more than just believing. Knowing that there is a force of energy that is present beyond us is definitely worth exploring.

When healing energies such as Urevia–Reiki–Karuna–etc., flow through our bodies, they connect us to the magical world of universal healing life-force energy and the energetic levels of our beings, our souls. Daily life and stress blocks the connection and communication with our higher self or soul, which is a precious resource of guidance, love, and energy for each person. This connection is vital for making positive choices and creating one's life experience. Healing energy supports the connection between the conscious mind, heart, and soul by reestablishing this link. It merges our spiritual world with our physical existence, supporting the expansion of our consciousness and well-being.

When our life's journey and our soul are in harmony, we experience great health and contentment. Many people are struggling with the current state of life on earth, making their anxiety and stress levels high. We have the power to help ourselves heal by using healing energies. They are not a religion or doctrine. It isn't necessary for a person to believe in healing energy to take advantage of its benefits.

It's all about one truth: Energy created us and energy is what we need for happiness, health, and empowerment. Everything we do each day involves energy: every thought, every choice, every action or inaction, every feeling, etc. requires life force energy. We give and receive energy from each other with every interaction. A healing practitioner simply channels high vibrations of spiritually guided life-force energy to a client, leaving him or her nourished, balanced, and recharged. In this state of harmony, the body restores its health and the mind, heart, and soul reconnect, removing mental and emotional clutter. Intuition, love, and clarity are enhanced, resulting in wiser choices and positive actions.

We can believe in the possibilities, and to have faith in the concept that there are greater things at work more powerful than all of humanity. After all, we are living on a planet floating in a giant solar system that is a micro dot compared to the universe. This life force energy is greater than we can image, and we are a part of it. It is through our connection with this greater energy that we heal, thrive, and create our best life.

Our attitude and the choices we make from moment to moment shape the energy of our life path and our daily experiences. If we don't like our life experience, then we need to make different choices. The choices can be big, small, serious, or light. As long as it's a positive difference, it doesn't matter. Even the smallest change or choice gradually accumulates with time, manifesting emotional and mental intentions.

If we believe in nothing except what we see before us, we still understand that each life is a chain of experiences that creates who we are. These chains of experience are in our control. Childhood has taught most of us we have the power to only respond to the world, and during childhood, that may have been true. As adults, we have more power to say 'Yes' or 'No.' To take back the power of choice is to take back the power to create.

Such a small thing in so many ways, but we have so much that holds us back from making choices that actually bring change to our life. Fear is the main reason we judge or block new possibilities or experiences. We're so terrified of losing control and venturing into uncharted territory that we rarely do anything. The dread of being incorrect and consequently feeling miserable is so powerful that we cannot act. In that moment, we give our power to situations, assume beliefs, and others around us, supporting their agendas rather than our own.

In our minds, we make every decision our final destination, and that is why we fear something new. The process we use is flawed. If we can remember that each choice leads us to another crossroads, and then another, we wouldn't fear truths that are different. We wouldn't fear new information. Instead, we would be open to new experiences and the opportunities they bring.

Say "Yes!" to new information and "Yes!" to action. We evolve in all ways. As we change, so do our living habits and spirituality. Each of us needs to gather those truths from our past that resonate with our hearts and move forward along our path, constantly reviewing our truths and how they apply in the present.

Healing energy, which is part of the universal life force energy, is a powerful resource. It helps to heal any issue or struggle that negatively affects the body, mind, and spirit. What is the explanation for this? Easy; human beings are made of life force energy and since we are energy beings, healing energy works. Everything we are, do, think, feel, create extends from our being. There is no life without energy and when stress or struggle disrupts the natural flow of energy in the aura, it compromises well-being and health.

Let us embrace new experiences like healing sessions or classes and give ourselves the opportunity to decide from personal knowledge whether it has value. Our emotions and our experiences are linked. Belief alone is not enough to make the right choice and create positive intentions. Heal yourself and share your gifts in order to take ownership of your health and life.

"CHANGE IS A CONSTANT FORCE: RELEASING THE OLD ENERGY TO MAKE ROOM FOR THE NEW."

Parable Two
Journal Entry

"Change"

I've been asked, "What is your truth?" When I hear those words, several things pop into my head all at once and none of them are precise. Sometimes my own beliefs confuse me. It's like a friend calling me on the phone and asking, "What's up?" So many things have happened

*since I have spoken to them last. I don't know
where to begin.*

*Everything is moving so fast around me, I can
barely keep up. Emotionally, I feel overwhelmed
by my changes and the world's struggle. The
other night, I was making dinner, and I started
crying out of pure frustration. The struggle of
trying to keep the details of life afloat is
exhausting. As I gather more information and
become an active participant in my world, its
pain brings me down to my knees and I feel
guilty about my self-pity. Then I say to myself,
'You have nothing to complain about compared
to so and so across the street and across the
ocean.' What do I do with all of this energy?*

*When I asked for spiritual growth and I prayed
for my path to be shown to me, I really didn't
understand the emotional floodgates that would
release and the resulting change within me. Some
emotional changes are so subtle, I barely feel them
until the outcome; then others are so intense, I feel*

*as if I have drowned in my own feelings. I am
Seeker, and I feel as if I have just stumbled. No,
that's not it. I feel as if a giant boulder has fallen
from the mountain above and parked itself dead
center on my life path. Taunting me to stop, listen,
and damn it all, feel. Feel everything: my past, my
present, and my feeling of uncertainty about my
future.*

*To help myself, I have been practicing the
healing hand positions once a week on a friend who
has agreed to be my guinea pig. I'm feeling energy
coming out of my hands and sense energy around
others and myself. Of course, I'm still doubting and
questioning if it's my imagination, but I am
committed to the learning process. I also noticed
that my friend has trouble with headaches, and
when I finish her treatment, the headache is gone
and she feels very relaxed.*

*Since I have felt nothing weird or bad yet, I am
going to take the next level of training. So far, when*

I pray and meditate, I feel more centered, which helps me reduce my daily stress. Although the techniques from the healing class seem helpful, the more I focus on my well-being, the more I am emotionally triggered by the surrounding people. This is a little disconcerting, because when I was keeping things as status quo, I wasn't feeling so responsive to others. So far, the journey feels soothing and stressful at the same time.

During the class, there was a guided angel meditation. I thought that maybe this technique would help bring me some clarity about my feelings. My first experience with the angel meditation was brief and clouded. The teacher was guiding our visualization, and I kept fidgeting, listening to the breathing pattern of the person next to me, and getting distracted by someone coughing from across the room. I wasn't very impressed with my experience, but I still felt guided to pursue it once I arrived home.

I waited until I was alone, turning on some calming music and lighting prayer candles. With my journal on my lap, I closed my eyes. Breathing deeply, I let my mind wander until I got bored. Eventually, after a few moments, my mind was ready to begin the visualization I learned in class.

Counting down from five to one, I entered a garden created by my imagination. It's too hard to see the entire garden all at once, so I shift my focus to a sitting area in the center of the garden. With my mind, I see myself sit down on a bench.

'Here comes the hard part.' I think to myself. I'm supposed to call my angel guide to me without trying too hard to make contact. 'Just let it happen, just let it happen. Don't force it.' I look down at my feet in the visualization because they are easy to see. Then I say a prayer asking for my angel to come to me.

'One, two, three, okay look up.' Gradually I look up and in my mind I see a fuzzy ball of white light. Physically, I feel a slight change in the surrounding energy, enough to know it isn't all in my head. As I continue to look at the light, a barefoot male figure in a pair of jeans and a button down flannel shirt emerges. He has light brown hair and average looks. I think to myself, 'Where are the wings and flowing robes?'

Hearing my thoughts, he smiles. Sitting down beside me, he says, "You can call me Ryan."

The first thing that pops into my head is 'Even his name is boring.'

This time he laughs out loud and says, "I take on the appearance that will be most comfortable and familiar to you without causing any fear."

"Oh," I sigh.
"Are you from the light?"

Glowing with white light, he replies, "Yes."

"What is your purpose with me?"

"To help you heal." Then he extended his arm towards the sky. "Look."

Looking up, I see an Eagle soaring over the garden. 'Oh boy,' I think, 'now my ego is really getting out of hand.'

Looking at me, he said, "You are like that eagle."

"What do you mean, I'm like the eagle? I don't understand?"

"The eagle is strong, intelligent, and perceptive. It is an animal totem that represents learning, intuition, and wisdom. You were meant to make the journey of personal growth to unlock your Divinity.

Sighing, I looked down at my hands. "I am afraid of change," I whispered. "If I grow, how will that affect my relationships, my life, my beliefs?" "How do I get rid of this fear that haunts my every thought?"

"By taking one step at a time with fear at your side, learning and gathering knowledge. As you gain in experience and wisdom, with time, your fear is gradually transformed into understanding and love,"

"I need to think about this." I got up from the bench. Ryan smiled with an understanding look on his face and waved "Good bye." I ended the visualization by taking a deep breath in, then opening my eyes on the exhale.

'Eagle.' I must have been projecting onto the visualization. My ego was probably getting in the way. The meditation was short and sweet, but I wanted time to process the experience. It wasn't

what I expected. I thought for sure I would see an angel with wings or something. Perhaps it was for the best. By not seeing an angel the first time, I can have some confidence in knowing that I didn't make it all up. If I had, there definitely would have been angel wings. I will try again in a few more weeks and see what happens.

A part of me feels like I am making the whole thing up in some desperate need to connect with the Divine. My teacher told me that our Spirit guides use our memories, thoughts, and familiar symbols to communicate messages. It is usually a simple message and feels like a thought popping into our head as if we were talking to ourselves. Some say it's the higher mind or higher-self communicating and that it is part of us. My teacher said it was a combination of both. I decided I don't care as long as it's accurate and comes from a divine source. My doubtful thoughts question if it's possible for me to access a greater knowledge without projecting my hidden anxieties or aspirations into the dialogue with my spiritual guides. How will I know for sure? How will I know divine guidance from ego or fear projection?

The only thing I can do is wait and see if, over time, my internal guidance is accurate. I will journal my experiences and look back on them after six months have passed and see if I can find any patterns of truth in the messages I gather during meditation.

A few weeks have passed since my first angel guide meditation attempt. When I came home for the day, I turned into my driveway, stopping briefly to pick up the mail and there was a cardboard gift box for me. It's from a childhood friend I haven't spoken to in several years. Surprised and delighted, I park my car in the garage and rush inside the house.

Taking my coat off, I sit down at the kitchen table and open my gift. I am so excited because a gift out of the blue is my favorite kind. Pushing the protective bubble wrap aside, I pull out a crystal eagle landing on a rock with its head bowed in respect. Tears come to my eyes immediately and I feel love, assurance, and joy all at the same time. Taking out the card, I read, "Ran into your mother the other day and she gave me your address. Shortly after, I saw this eagle in a shop, and for some reason, I thought of you. I hope you like it. With love, your friend."

I couldn't believe it! Falling down to my knees, I looked up and said, "Thank you! I needed this confirmation more than I realized."

I place the eagle on my prayer altar to remind me to have faith in myself, in Spirit, and in the process. **What a miracle!**

Chapter Two
The Relationship between Change and Miracles

The universal law of Cause and Effect has linked
'the experience of change' with 'the manifestation
of miracles' in a complicated dance. One cannot be
present without the other. We usually see miracles
as God's response to prayers for a blessing and
that's true. We rarely consider our soul has to be
willing and ready to receive the miracle in the first
place to allow for co-creation. This means we need
to be emotionally and mentally ready first to create
a window of opportunity for the miracle to
manifest, such as asking for help and be willing to
receive that gift without worry. If we want our

spiritual lives to fall into place, we must be open to the energy of change.

There are no wrong choices because our decisions result from our evolution. We cannot evolve without growth, and we cannot grow without new experiences. We need to expand our belief system and update it as we develop. As we make new decisions, motivated by learning and wisdom, the universal law of Cause and Effect represents those changes, and when those changes manifest, we experience miracles.

It is important to have the intention to create miracles, especially when we feel unsatisfied with our life. When we feel stuck, repetitive, and heavy, it's time to pause and assess. To understand what needs changing, we need to look at our unsatisfied feelings. Being honest about self-sabotage is the first step in co-creating miracles with the Divine.

Our feelings, not our logic, have the power to manifest miracles. We access the pathway of wisdom through our emotional needs that are not being honored by ourselves. Our repressed fear, anger, and resentment are chains that bind us. We don't have to understand why we feel the way we do; we just need to be willing to move on and embrace change. Change creates growth, and growth creates happiness.

It's challenging to release our assumptions, particularly when we think things are simply the way they are and that's that. Human beings usually let go in stages, gradually getting ready for something new. Moving forward becomes more desirable than holding on to the status quo. The question is, where do we go? Whether the transition is emotional, physical, or both, it is uncomfortable. People are reluctant to let go and make changes because of the discomfort they associate with it.

Miracles happen when we seek, ask, need, let go, change, and participate in the process of co-creation. Miracles cannot manifest in our lives if we do not take part in the experience or take the needed action. We should be prepared to contribute to our own well-being while we seek Divine support. Every experience is to gather information and understanding that will guide us towards personal happiness and wellbeing. Our life path, our spiritual path, is designed perfectly for each individual's gifts, lesson, growth, empowerment, and happiness, so embrace the content of the day even if undesirable; trust and work with the energy, process it, and move on.

Fear causes us to ignore our needs and dreams, resulting in a reality of deprivation. Life then lacks love, happiness, and success. Living a healthy life requires us to receive, ask for help, use the surrounding resources, and make changes. We cannot create miracles if we are unwilling to participate and rise above lower vibrations. It's every soul's responsibility to have a positive impact on others and this world. To make this happen, one needs to work through their own issues and their relationships with others.

Of course, the lessons within our relationships spread out to our spirituality, our careers, and to the planet therefore, everything is affected. The law of Cause and Effect is about creating positive energy in our relationships with others: wishing only the best for others. Over time, that positive energy gradually manifests in all areas of our life, creating a happy life experience.

Sometimes We Need Help:

We empower miracles through intention and ceremony. A ceremony can be something as small as sitting in front of a prayer altar each day, saying a prayer and lighting a candle or performing full moon creation ceremonies to connect with the creative energy of the universe. People often observe a full moon ceremony at night when the moon is at its fullest, and this practice can be repeated for several months. During each ceremony, the angels and the four elements are asked to be present and provide guidance. Then a candle is lit, while a person states his or her intention. Using a piece of paper, he or she writes the intention on a piece of paper. Then light the paper with the candle flame to start the paper burning. Set the paper in a burning bowl and requesting the smoke carry the prayer or intention to Spirit. Allow the candle to stay lit until it's gone, or snuff out the flame and light it up again every day until there's nothing left.

This ritual can be done every full moon until healing and reconciliation is reached.

Making peace with yourself in this lifetime can be useful. This includes your personality traits and your nature. How do you know who that person is? Your heart's desire is being that person. It is the behaviors and activities that bring you contentment. What comes naturally to you? The gifts that come with your natural personality are effortless to share. Stop, feel, and listen to what you want and need to do for happiness and success. This method will make you familiar with your current self, which will alter as time passes. If you're not at that point yet, then just take one step forward and make a tiny change somewhere in your life and miracles will follow.

*"USE AND SHARE
WHAT HAS BEEN
GIVEN TO YOU, AND IN
THE SHARING,
ABUNDANCE FLOWS –
LIFEFORCE FLOWS."*

Parable Three
Journal Entry

"Love, Courage, & Wisdom"

Before the healing class, I didn't make the connection between my everyday feelings and my spiritual evolution. "I'm spiritual." I say to myself. Of course I am. I believe in God. I have faith. I pray all the time and I am a good person. Then why am I so angry? It's not a roaring in my ears kind of anger, but a subtle ho-hum anger of

"I'm fine, everything's fine, but don't bother me. I don't have the energy to deal with this and you too." Work is okay. The house hasn't fallen down yet. I have friends. Family. Well, everyone has a family. What am I supposed to improve? Isn't this the way life is? You live, you love as best as you can, you work, and you die. What do I need to improve? I don't need to change. Things are okay the way they are. I don't have any complaints. Life is as it should be, right?

The more I meditate and the more I expand my awareness of the energy around me, the more emotionally sensitive I become. I am missing the old days of self-denial and ignorance. It's harder for me to let things go. I want to stop the other person from mistreating me. I want to say "Hey! What did you just say to me?" The urge to fight or hide is stronger. These issues have always hurt my feelings, but I either flip the argument around on the other person for protection, or I stew on it and talk to my friends about it. I can't find the words to tell the person who caused me harm.

This anger is bringing me down. I don't want this emotional drama in my life. It's not like I have problems every day; just when I get into an argument, someone says something rude, or when I feel exposed, embarrassed, or stupid.

I'm aware of the subtle emotional dynamics between myself and the people I'm interacting with, and I can see the areas that need to change, however I'm not enthusiastic about it. I don't want to tackle the patterns in my relationships. Things are okay as they are. I'm not sure if changing my self is worth the effort. When I signed up for a healing class, it was so that I could learn something new in the realm of spiritual expression. I didn't bargain for the emotional and mental changes to be part of the package. The class wasn't the exact cause of the transformation, but something inside me has changed and, as a result, I am looking for more. Of what, I'm not exactly sure; other than I am drawn to the serenity that I feel when I harmonize with the energy around me.

I feel thrown off by the people around me. Yeah, that's it. I would be fine if people didn't disagree with me and lived up to my expectations. Oops, I slipped into my dream world again. Pardon me.

Since I can't control the other people in my environment, perhaps, I should deal with my anger. It could be easier to keep my triggers in check if my anger hasn't been accumulating inside me, ready to be set off by the slightest provocation. If I'm honest with myself, people frustrate me more than I like. I struggle with the fact that when I am angry; I want to say something mean or just leave. I don't want to take the time to sit and ask, "Why?"

Well, maybe my angels have some advice for me. I don't want to be victimized by my anger. It's creating a lot of tension, a slight feeling of depression, and an automatic reaction any time someone says something I don't appreciate.

Sitting with my journal, I close my eyes and prepare myself for meditation. I take deep breaths while I am counting back from five to one and immediately I see myself sitting on the bench in the garden. Ryan is there, sitting on the bench next to me, with a patient look in his eyes.

"Hi, Ryan"

He smiles, "Welcome, Seeker. I am glad you have created a connection with us today. I want to introduce two new spiritual beings today."

Sweeping his arm towards the right, I follow the motion with my eyes. I see a White sphere of light directly in front of the oak tree in the North position of the garden. Stepping from the light, I see a Native American Indian with long white hair and white leather clothes. I think, 'Oh, what a cliché. Everyone sees a Native American spirit guide.' The Indian walks up to me and I can see that he is old with an eagle feather braided in his hair by his right temple. He smiles, "My name is White Eagle." I just smile back and nod my head.

White Eagle sits down next to Ryan. "You have much to learn, and your true path is just beginning."

"What do you mean, my true path?"
"Well, the path that leads you to your true self."

"I thought I was my true self already. I mean, I know who I am." 'At least I think I do,' I silently add to myself.

"You think you know who you are, but you do not have all the information to make an informed

decision. Soon, however, you will understand that you are living a life that is too small for who you really are."

"And who is that?"

White Eagle smiled, shifted his position and extended his legs so that he could cross his ankles. Leaning back, he casually says, "You need to spend time near the water."

"Ok, water, got it. How does that answer my question?"

"As you walk through your life, the answers will unfold for you. We can only guide you; we cannot tell you who you are. You will discover that for yourself. We can give you tools to help; I am suggesting that you start with water, preferably the ocean."

Ryan stands up, drawing my attention to him, and reaches for my hand. Bringing me to a standing position, he turns me towards a glowing ball of white light that entered the garden. "Go to the light, Seeker." I step forward and I am overwhelmed with emotion. I feel something from this light. Looking closer, I see a figure with wings, and holding my breath, I see an Angel walk towards me. Her face is welcoming and loving. I feel very safe. She steps closer to me and hugs me.

"I am your guardian Angel, Seeker, and I am with you always. I have three gifts for you on this day. They are love, courage, and wisdom." Stepping back, she blows out her breath and a swirling wind fills me with a sparkling mist. I could feel the healing power of her gifts. It felt so good.

With gratitude over flowing from my heart, I whisper, "Thank you." She acknowledges my statement with a slight tilt of her head, and then she turns back into a white ball of light that gradually disappears.

Beaming like a little kid, I turn back to Ryan and White Eagle. "Did you see what she gave me?"

They smiled. "That is enough for today, Seeker. Return your consciousness to your reality and write about your experience." I waved goodbye, let go of the visual in my mind, and focused on my breathing and the weight of my body.

*Back to normal consciousness, I think; I finally saw some wings. I'm in a good place, but I don't understand what love, courage, and wisdom really signify in practical terms. I'm still struggling to find a way to modify my behavior to reduce strife and discord. White Eagle said to work with water. Well, I don't live anywhere near an ocean, but in class, the teacher suggested sea salt baths to help clear out imbalanced energy. I will start with that, and I will schedule a healing session, so I can **process my anger and see what it has to say.**

Chapter Three

Anger

If anger is used to cause pain, either indirectly through manipulation, or directly through hurtful words, it is a destructive force, creating more negativity. If, however, it's used as a guide — as a gateway to self-discovery and unconscious fears/insecurities — it's a catalyst for change.

Where does fear come from? Fear is a by-product of being born into or creating a lifestyle that doesn't support our needs or our individual nature. Questioning our value due to self-doubt can keep us from allowing ourselves to create and live the life we want instead of adhering to the conventional nine-to-five way of life. To create a lifestyle that is supportive of our needs on the heart level, we need to discover our values and passions. It's usually easy to recognize and incorporate values into one's life, however, they should be updated if necessary. Don't assume that your level of happiness at thirty will remain the same or decrease when you reach sixty.

Passions are a call to action: something that speaks to the heart, and a person feels the need to take action, even if it is challenging. If you don't know what you are passionate about, pay attention to the things that trigger your anger, and ask yourself, "Why am I angry?" An unsatisfying life can bring on feelings of anger. Anger is telling you that you have dishonored yourself or let someone else dishonor you by the choices you have made. We put ourselves in a corner by how we set things up. Any of the multiple possibilities can service every person's needs. Our mental and emotional imprints have a tendency to repeat childhood programming and assumption instead of using creative problem-solving skills to find positive solutions. Fear of change and taking responsibility for creating that change is a powerful blocking force for some.

There's no need to feel scared because utilizing the gifts we have been given and expressing our passions with others or asking for help meets our requirements and long-term contentment, which realizes our soul's life purpose. Everyone's mission on the planet is the same: transforming our fear and living our Divinity. Our life purpose is our individual expression of the Divine within. We identify our life purpose by listening to what the anger is trying to tell us about ourselves, transforming fear and setting wisdom free. With healing, we gain in strength and clarity. If we understand what we want but still find it difficult to bring our life purpose into reality, more healing is necessary.

Repressing anger creates resentment, bitterness, and judgment. In doing so, it blocks the heart with fear, and limits connection to the soul. When we don't tap into the power of our Divinity, we tend to feel lost, without direction, and become anxious.

The worry leads to more anger because we feel out of control. The smallest things will trigger our emotional defenses. Internally, the tension builds and we become tired. Being tired leads to stress and stress leads back to anger. As this vicious circle revolves and gains momentum, depression sets in along with hopelessness.

What is the resolution? First, we admit to being angry and we listen. We grow by using the passion that anger stirs up. Our passion drives us to look within before we become overwhelmed with worry and fatigue.

Second, we look at the bigger picture and let go of victimhood belief systems or imprints. We must realize we have power in the situation before we can claim it. We can either choose to live in fear and as victims, or to choose the path of truth and love.

Third, we must confront our rage to truly comprehend how we trap ourselves in emotional predicaments. Then we can track how we set it up and created the unfavorable outcome that caused the anger to begin with. Facilitators are especially useful in this region. Being uninvolved emotionally will enable them to view the circumstances in a more lucid way.

The fourth step is to understand the difference between compromise and adapting. It's always possible to come to a compromise through negotiation, and adapting internally is a way to avoid any strife. Compromising is the energy you want to work with. Adapting and dishonoring your needs will only create resentment and anger. Facing our fear around conflict, communicating without blame, staying in the "I need, I feel," discussing issues, negotiating change, and following through with action will transform negative relationship conflict patterns.

We can modify our own behavior to transform our anger internally without involving someone else. Most issues do not need to be discussed with the individual person who is triggering the feelings. When we understand our feelings and decide what we need to do internally, it's often all that is needed. Paying attention to how we set things up, using boundaries, and understanding the needs of others is a healthy way to process our anger. Sometimes people or situations do not change, and in these moments, we need to take responsibility for choosing the circumstances. The question becomes, "Is the investment of our energy and time worth the long-term return?"

"YOU KNOW YOU ARE ON THE RIGHT PATH- MAKING THE RIGHT CHOICES - WHEN YOU FEEL CONTENT AND AT PEACE WITH SELF."

Parable Four
Journal Entry

"Processing"

The healing session was wonderful. I could feel the divine energy flowing through my body as the practitioner placed her hands on me. Lying on the healing/massage table, I felt heavy and light at the same time. As the energy flowed through my body, my muscles relaxed while my *cells absorbed the healing light. I could feel myself being filled from the inside out until I was a glowing ball of light. Relaxing further into the healing session, I felt the healing energy lift and clear the heavy, negative energy I had been carrying. I didn't realize how much until I felt it lift off of me.*

Getting off of the table, I felt relaxed, clear, balanced and light all at the same time. I was mentally clear, emotionally open and centered, and physically relaxed and grounded. Sitting in the chair across from the practitioner, I thought the healing session was the best thing I had ever experienced. I was ready to look within and "own" my power.

As I was processing my anger with the practitioner, I felt a fear come over me. What if I am being selfish by honoring my own needs? My anger was telling me I didn't like many things about my life and about the people around me. The more

I communicated my anger, the more I realized I wasn't living a life that expressed my value system. It was simply a matter of surviving emotionally and financially, and I was simply reacting to the circumstances.

I'm thinking, 'This sucks!!!' How do I heal this pattern? It is so natural I don't even know where to begin. Then, the practitioner drops another bomb on me, saying that anger held within for a long time in the second chakra, (lower belly), flows upward to the heart and creates resentment, blocking the flow of the Divine energy. Not stopping there, the resentment needs to be fed. Its negative vibration sends out a signal to the universe like a beacon, creating more experiences that fulfill its prophecy. The ego gets to feel like it is right, that it knows everything, and that we are indeed justified in our victimhood.

The practitioner went on further, saying that resentment becomes bitterness long term; so that as we age, we become rigid, judgmental, and unforgiving. This eventually disconnects us from all forms of love, leaving only pain.

"How do I even begin to heal?"

"As your practitioner, I am only a guide. How you heal and when you heal is up to you. I am here to listen, to ask the right questions, to provide guidance based upon your answers, to support you while you go through the process, and to provide clarity when needed. The first guidance I can give you is to stop trying to prove you are a good person worthy of love and approval from your family and peers."

"How do I do that?"

The practitioner leaned towards me, looked me in the eye and said, "Constantly giving, putting others first even in small, subtle ways is not only fear based, but a drain on your energy.

The only time such action is necessary is during a crisis, but it's not meant to be a lifestyle. This gradually creates fatigue, and you can't heal or change anything if you are tired. Healing requires change, and change requires energy. If you are waking up tired, you don't have enough energy to heal and create a happier life."

"So, how do I get more energy?"

"Well," the practitioner said, what makes you happy?" "What do you value?"

"I value alone time, walks in the woods, happy relationships, being a good and spiritual person, having a good home, being financially independent, reading, being healthy, meditation, and so on."

The practitioner leaned back. "I would start making life choices that create your value system. I would start doing the things that make you happy. Let go of some control, ask for help, and receive."

My fear of being selfish was creeping up again, and I needed to tell the practitioner. "It feels selfish to me to do what I want to do when there are so many things I need to do."

"We worry about being selfish, but when we are unhappy, tired, frustrated, stressed, angry, and then bitter, we become the person we are trying to prevent: withholding and short-tempered. In doing so, we become what we fear — the lower version of ourselves. **When we are tired, we exhibit selfish behavior. When we enjoy life, we have energy. Happy people effortlessly give more.** *If you want to be a good person, enjoy your life and the rest will balance itself out in the long run. It is easier to connect to the Divine when our heart chakra is not full of repressed anger."*

The practitioner stands up. "That is enough for today. Go home, absorb the information and do one thing a day that is in alignment with your value system."

I reach out and give the practitioner a hug and say, "Thank you."

*As I'm driving home, I feel overwhelmed with the information, and I am still angry. There are unhappy situations that I have experienced with others that are still bothering me. I'm not sure I will handle the demands placed on me by life and still have enough energy left over to create my heart's desire. Oops, I'm doing it again. I need to redirect my thoughts. I focus on self-care first and others second unless there is a crisis or great need. Except, what if their needs conflict with mine, or if we have a difference of opinions on an issue that cannot be ignored? The practitioner advised to stop adjusting and concentrate on negotiation. Every disagreement must **be discussed** until a solution is found that both parties can accept.*

*But what if we are on opposing sides of an issue and we value different things? **How do I stand in***

my power and let others do the same when
conflicting belief systems or needs are present?

Chapter Four

Power

Doubt leads to fear, fear to insecurity, which leads to anger and misuse of power. Our power is everything we think, do, say, or don't do. Basically, every conscious and unconscious decision we make expresses our chi or personal power. Now why should personal power be an issue? It's not, except for one area in our lives: relationships. We spend most of our lives interacting with relationships, which means power is a big deal. Relationships are a primary source of love, happiness, or pain. Goddess/God gave us all equal power, and equal need for each other, which explains why we are highly motivated to have relationships despite their difficultly and energy investment.

We all have emotional triggers or insecurities: unresolved negative feelings from childhood that we carry into adulthood. When a person or situation ignites our insecurities/fears, the most common first defense is anger, then control and closing off or shutting down–effectively putting up a wall of defense. It's wiser to change the pattern and learn what is the right choice or action for each situation gradually accumulating positive energy thereby, creating a happier, healthier future. Most people experience five stages of power, but there are three things we need to understand before we even get to the first stage of power.

The three things that prepare us for the five stages of power are: knowing what keeps you centered, knowing what your triggers are, and knowing what tools work for you in a difficult situation.

Living a lifestyle that keeps us centered is one of the best things we can do to handle times of growth, for example, exercise, eating right, relaxation, etc.

Knowing what triggers us is easy. Our history and memories highlight the issues we carry around. Situations that make us feel stupid, embarrassed, nervous, not good enough as we are, abandoned or threatened push our hot buttons. Knowing the triggers and how we respond is important. We may become aggressive, talk too much to prove ourselves, be overly sensitive, and close our heart and respond from the head only.

Once we understand our sensitivities more, we also need to identify the tools or emotional social skills that keep us focused, centered, and wise. For example, pausing before we speak, taking deep breaths, and truly listening to self and others. From here, you are ready to work with the first stage of power.

POWER STAGE ONE:

AWARENESSS OF PERSONAL POWER
At this level, we take responsibility for our reality, our half of relationships, and our personal feelings. We stand in our power and realize what it means. We do not expect others to save us, make it better, or make us happy. It no longer feels satisfying to justify victimhood. The ego matures.

POWER STAGE TWO:

THE TERRIBLE TWOS
Our fear motivates us to be aggressive, defensive, or protective when challenged by others at this level: to protect us from feeling pain or uncomfortable emotions. We are controlling of our environment and sometimes others, such as the lifestyle of a household. We have a "mine-mine" attitude about our space, our things, our family, etc. We believe we are right most of the time and can be emotionally and mentally stubborn or self-righteous. When we begin our healing path, we flow back and forth between stages one and two.

As more wisdom is gathered, we incorporate stage three.

POWER STAGE THREE:

BALANCED POWER
We realize how our actions and decisions affect others. We learn the right action of power by remembering who we want to be and using discernment situation by situation, considering each one as unique. With the power of negotiation, we create balance. We are still protective at this level, but less threatened by someone else's words, how they feel about us, decisions, beliefs, etc.

POWER STAGE FOUR:

QUIET POWER
We no longer feel the need to justify our decisions and prove our value. We allow the results of our actions to speak for themselves. We are comfortable with our personal belief systems and choices. We are peaceful and happy with our lifestyle. We understand the true meaning of freedom.

POWER STAGE FIVE:

ONENESS OF POWER - ANGELIC STAGE
We reach this stage during meditation and living a balanced, loving life promoting goodwill as much as possible. When we are happy, we can maintain this level of awareness more often in our lives. Our

self-love issues are healed. Our mind is flexible and our heart is compassionate. We have wisdom, vision, and we understand the bigger picture in all situations. We also understand the true meaning of power/love, right action, compassion, higher wisdom, and our fears are processed in a healthy way, transforming the negative energy they generate. The aura stays strong, open, and fluid, promoting health, spirituality, and well-being.

We can use the five stages of power as a guide. It may take us several years to attain all five and remain at the upper levels. We can be comforted by the fact that we gain a lot from progressing through the stages and none of our efforts are wasted. The Angels rejoice in our courage.

Learning to live above our lower vibrations– tendencies or lower version of our-self is not always easy. The Angels know Earth is the free will zone. At anytime, we can turn our backs on healing our issues and ignore our purpose for being here, and in all truth, some do. The Angels cannot interfere with free will choice, so they have faith in us, and each day trust that we will keep going even when we are dead, dog-tired. Just as we need to trust them and have faith that they will help us. No matter how difficult our struggles may be, we will still be taken care of during our lifetime.

Our truth, our mission, is the realization of perfection in thy form. We are here to live fully, to love and be loved. Our personality is designed perfectly for our life experience. We can trust our natural personality and gifts. Even though we are flawed, we still have value. A person could wait forever for validation from others. It's wiser to accept self and live a good life. Happy, self-aware, kind people are not fearful and angry. They don't punish, control, or inflict pain on others.

Earth's reality is a paradox. We are born to parents who are struggling with their own truth, and many do not know how to live a life that teaches their children the skills needed for a healthy self and life. The reality we are born into programs and imprints our consciousness with belief systems that are contrary to our soul's truth. This contrast, in truth, creates insecurities, self-doubt, and we spend our lives trying to prove ourselves. Fear motivates the behavior, creating more emotional dissatisfaction.

We have to uncover who we are beneath all the indoctrination, and be the individual that lives within. That is the key to happiness. Sometimes standing in our truth or identity is very difficult because we have relationships with others who have yet to find that for themselves. This can make others feel threatened by us or project their insecurities/fears onto us. It is important that we do not let someone else's fears, beliefs, or opinions create self-doubt. The only question we need to ask is, "Based on my intuition, what is the right action to take at this time?" The answer will vary from situation to situation or even as time passes and as a person strengthens in wisdom.

How do we stand in our truth when others are projecting their insecurities/fears onto us? We make conscious decisions that express our highest potential and use our words carefully. Wise and respectful communication is the pathway of integrity. Knowing what to say, when to say it, when to be silent, and when to listen are very important factors in life.

Wise communication requires a person to stop pretending that we are something more than ourselves. We often pretend we are more important, more intelligent, more loving, rather than just knowing we are perfect as we are. We do not trust our goodness and we worry about every action.

Self-worth issues create shadows or negative emotional patterns that the ego expresses through anger, fear, insecurities, or exhaustion. Shadows or patterns are a composite of denied emotions that are fear based and therefore, block intuition and clarity. When our natural intuition is blocked, it's hard to know what to do or how to speak with wisdom. This is a vicious cycle that creates hurt feelings and unresolved issues.

To take this healing further, we need to work with the negative emotional patterns as they come up. With time, our communication skills improve and as they improve, our Divinity/Integrity manifests through the way we communicate and actions we take. Now, just because we are trying to live with emotional integrity doesn't mean everyone else is. To help us work with other people, it is beneficial to remember who we are and who we want to be. It is also helpful to be clear about what we will give and not give, always keeping in mind the individuals we are dealing with and their capabilities.

Emotional contracts listing expectations and boundaries keep everyone on the same page. They are not for everyone, but emotional contracts can be a good place to start if a person is still learning how to communicate with integrity and wisdom. These contracts, also known as mediation, are verbalized, sometimes written; there is a behavior accountability clause. Why do we need to go through all this trouble you may ask? Because to expect everyone to be in their integrity and do the right thing when they are emotionally triggered is an unrealistic expectation. Research has shown that when our anger passes a certain threshold, the problem solving part of our brain shuts down. The survival, instinctual part of our brain turns on. When this happens, we are past the point of resolution. Unless someone has done a lot of emotional growth, it is almost impossible to do the right thing when the fearful/defense patterns have been engaged. That is not a bad thing, it is just a fact of human nature and it helps us learn and grow. With maturity and emotional wisdom, most people improve.

To heal, we need to take responsibility (power stage one) for the relationship patterns we have co-created up to this point, and as a result, what personal needs are being ignored or repressed. Negotiating action plans that work for both parties creates change and transforms negative patterns.

What do we do when the other person isn't willing to take on half the responsibility of the relationship by being accountable and reaching agreements that are beneficial for both of us? It might be possible to solve the issue by making some personal choices that promote self-care in the situation and see if that is enough; some issues are resolved by simply accepting what is or taking responsibility for personal happiness. If that is not enough to balance the energy, ask the person for help in creating a better relationship. If they say, "No," and they are not family, decide if the relationship is working for you as it is. Then decide if the unresolvable issues are too difficult to accept. If so, take responsibility and make a change.

If you have a problem with a close family relative and you value family, but they are unwilling to negotiate resolutions, then you need to decide what your boundaries are and make some internal commitments to self. By honoring your needs in the situation, even if the family member doesn't want, or know how to, it will improve the relationship with time. Always respect yourself without seeking approval for your needs and feelings. Treat your family with respect and work with the personality clashes as best as you can and let the rest go.

As we live our lives, we have several opportunities, large and small, to realize our needs. Something triggers our anger when our needs in the situation are not being meant. Ask yourself, "What do I need in this situation to feel comfortable?" Feeling comfortable is a good place to start.

While we are in the middle of our own stuff and trying to communicate clearly without blame, there are some helpful tools we can use to improve our emotional social skills.

Communication Tools

1. Mean what you say and say what you mean.
2. Take the time to (feel) before you speak and give yourself permission to take a break and come back to the person later; time offers clarity and emotional balance.
3. Be honest with yourself and be clear about your emotional motivation.
4. Communicate without blame and take responsibility for your feelings.
5. Don't apologize for your feelings or prove their value. Our feelings are always valuable because we are.
6. Ask for what you want.

7. Keep your expectations realistic and be conscious of the other person's personality and needs.

8. Be willing to take responsibility for your own happiness.

9. Don't try to fix, care-take, or protect others from their issues. This will only enable dependency.

10. Acknowledge and value the other person's needs as your own because you value your relationship with them.

Listening is just as important as speaking.

1. Repeat back to the person what you hear them say, especially the intention and emotional needs you are picking up from the conversation.

2. Respect the position or point of view even if you do not agree with it.

3. Address the emotional needs you are hearing.

4. Listen in total support and look for common ground.

5. Ask the person, "What do you really want? Are you sure you want it?" "What are you afraid of experiencing?" "How does this improve your life?" "How will this make you happy?"

6. Do not make it about being right or wrong. Everyone's feelings are valuable and need to be honored.

Responding to what you hear coming from others is important.

1. Start with saying "I hear you."
2. Breathe and stay calm in the face of criticism. Remember, understanding their point of view does not mean you agree with it.
3. Be willing to think about what they are saying, even if you do not agree, and be honest with what you can and cannot do long-term.
4. Ask for specific feedback.
5. Respond by saying something like, "I will think about it or I will consider it and get back to you."
6. If conflict begins, backtrack and ask, "When you say so and so, what do you mean by that, or can you repeat that again?" You may need to take a break and get back to the person later on this point, or if you continue to communicate, ask the other person to say in one sentence what it is that they want and you do the same. Then work on an action plan together that allows both people to get what they want. Please do not debate about who is right and who is wrong. It is a relationship, not a competition.

If an agreement cannot be created, then the question is, 'Is this relationship worth the long-term investment and can I let this go and still be happy?'

We need to keep our communication in alignment with our emotional integrity and be the person we want to be. Our words are one of the most powerful forces we have to manifest love and happiness.

"THE LIGHT WITHIN ME CALLS TO THE LIGHT WITHIN YOU TO HELP MAKE THIS A BETTER PLACE."

Parable Five
Journal Entry

"Standing in our Power"

Today I am going to have lunch with Terri. I am excited to tell someone about my healing path. I have been trying very hard to communicate clearly, and do something each day for balance and joy. I am feeling better making these minor changes since I realized I could still fulfill my daily obligations without giving up personal time. So, I am excited to take some time out of my schedule and have lunch with a good friend.

Later that day, Terri and I greet each other warmly at our favorite coffee shop and find a table by the window so we can enjoy the view. After ordering, we catch up on news and family stuff. Gradually, the conversation turns to my personal healing work.

"Terri, I say, I am excited to share with you about something that I have found very helpful. I am in the middle of taking some Metaphysical/Spiritual classes, and getting energy healing sessions regularly. It has been a lot of work, but I am feeling more balanced and peaceful."

"Really, what do you mean, classes and healings? I am unfamiliar with healing sessions."

"Well, um, the classes are designed to give you peaceful, self-healing techniques for well-being and spiritual growth as well as practitioner training, so you can also give a healing session to others. The

personal healing sessions are for detailed self-awareness that can't be covered in a group setting. The healing practitioner acts as a guide by helping you discover your own truth and wisdom."

Terri furrows her eyebrows. "I am not sure; it sounds pretty weird to me. Are you sure it's not evil or something?" Leaning in, Terri whispers, "Where does this healing energy come from? The Bible says Jesus can heal, but I have never heard of someone else being able to heal us. Are you sure that you aren't messing with some bad stuff? You should be careful; you might get yourself into trouble. Are you going to church?"

I am feeling uncomfortable and anxious. I take a deep breath in and calm my nerves. "When I first thought about taking the classes, I had the same concerns, but I decided I wanted to experience more. I love my church, but I needed more, and I didn't know exactly what that was, so I thought I would try to broaden my horizons. I also was very careful and gave myself permission to stop if I felt unsure. Besides, nobody else heals you; the individual heals themselves."

Across the table, Terri's furrowed brow turns into a scowl.

"Terri, it has been a wonderful experience for me. Metaphysical healing modalities are not religions, nor do they replace or interfere with an individual's religion. They teach you about love, about integrity, and how to use your personal power to contribute positive energy to the world around you. Goddess/God is believed to exist in everything and inside everyone. The classes encourage the individual to connect with his or her Divinity, complimenting and integrating with religious beliefs."

"However, there is one major difference that sets apart metaphysical healing modalities: There isn't any organized group that has rules or leadership.

Healing is considered an individual path. It is up to the person to create and define for him or herself. The metaphysical teachers are guides, but not leaders. It is up to the individual to merge his or her healing path with personal religious beliefs and create a supportive environment to live in. It is also interesting there are no specific beliefs we have to believe before we can heal personal issues.

"The metaphysical people that I have encountered believe in Goddess/God and Jesus. Metaphysics doesn't demand that you give up your religious beliefs or even demand that you change them. The only actual difference between the two is metaphysics reminds us that everything is energy; that we have a relationship with the life force energy that creates and surrounds us. We have the power to change our energy and because of that, the human experience is considered sacred and equal in value to Spirit. I have found my healing experience to be spiritually empowering."

Terri leans back, "Yeah, but what do you think about tarot, astrology and all those wacky psychics? The Bible says they are evil."

*"What version of the Bible are you talking about? After all, there are so many, not to mention the missing scripts that aren't even included in most of the different versions. The Bible is a composite of visions and stories. To be more specific, part of the Bible is **channeled information** by someone who claimed to have a vision or heard God's voice. Who is to say that it is accurate? Who is to say who can and cannot connect to God? The Bible has been re-written and modified several times. It is possible that certain visions or stories were altered for personal gain. It's hard to determine, based on the Bible alone, what options we have regarding how we connect with Goddess/God."*

"Tarot and astrology have been here for as long, if not longer, than the Bible. If we are pieces of Goddess/God, then it would make sense to me that we would develop some way to communicate with Spirit. These modalities are not better or worse than the channeled Bible,

which certain people have used for power and control. I have learned that everything has purpose and can be used in either a positive or negative way."

Terri sighs, "I don't know. I think we can use tarot for evil."

"I tell you what Terri, name one thing that can't be used for evil. All things are neutral until we decide with our intention how to use it. Humans make things good or bad. There are excellent doctors and there are bad ones. There are good psychics and there are bad ones. It is the same with all things in life. I do not believe that tarot taps into negativity unless the person using the cards has a lot of negative issues to work out. Yes, we must use discernment, but to project our fear onto things we don't understand isn't very Godly of us, is it? That is like saying, don't drive to work because you might get in an accident and cars are evil. I have learned that anything that serves my self-awareness

and helps me become more positive is useful. If the path leads towards love and good things, I walk it."

"Terri, please understand; I decided I would not let fear close me off from new perspectives or new information to simply consider; that I was going to use my wisdom to decide what was right for me. These classes are guiding me towards a loving place. For the first time in my life, I am standing in my power and letting my heart be my guide, not others."

Terri stands up and says, "Well, I need to get going. It was nice seeing you." Standing up, I reach out and say, Are you okay, Terri?" She shakes her head. "I don't know what I think about all of this. I don't know if I want to be around you if you are doing these things."

"But Terri, we don't have to have the same belief system to be friends. You are one of my dearest friends. I would like to continue our

friendship. I know you are worried about me, but isn't it possible that we can just see the goodness in each other and trust that the other person is doing what is right for them?"

"I don't know; I am uncomfortable talking about this metaphysical stuff. I would rather not be around it."

"We don't have to discuss it if it makes you feel uncomfortable. I was just sharing my life with you."

"Yeah, okay, I will talk to you later." Terri turned and walked out the door.

Arriving at home, I think to myself 'Boy, this standing in your own power is hard stuff." I can feel myself begin to doubt and wonder if I should have kept my mouth shut. I could lose a friendship over this, and if Terri tells more people, and they react in the same way, I could lose more than one *friend. I don't want to lose my social circle, but I also don't want to stop pursuing my path. This is hard! I need to have faith that **I am on the right path for myself.***

Chapter Five

I'm not in Trouble

"Oh, the fear of it all," our greatest weakness is the childhood programming that we are going to get into trouble if we don't do what we are supposed to do, or at least pretend we are doing it. Now, as adults, we may say, "No way, I am not worried about getting in trouble. I am in control of my own life. I do what I want to do." Really, are you sure?

Standing in our power can sometimes feel like we are going to get in trouble. We are not exactly sure from whom just that there is a sense that we might. Keep in mind, most of this automatic response will be subconscious, and we might have a hard time identifying this behavior at the moment it happens. This feeling motivates us to hide things, to defend ourselves against criticism, and to modify our behavior in certain situations. We don't want to expose any part of ourselves that may draw negative attention and gossip.

This lesson is one of the hardest we will ever learn: 'We are not in trouble from any force, human or otherwise.' Now, we are not talking about extremes such as murder, etc. That is more than unusual behavior, it's messed up negative behavior and it's a whole other story. The concepts discussed in this book are around relationships, both personal and professional.

We fear getting in trouble with our spouse, with our boss, with our family and friends. This fear is a powerful motivator in our lives. We know intellectually that we cannot be sent to the principal's office or sent to our room, yet the inner child still believes that it might be possible. As an adult, the fear translates into worry about losing our job, spouse, money, etc. Just because we are all grown up doesn't mean our past doesn't affect us. If it isn't other people we fear, then it's God or Spirit. If we sin, we will get in trouble, and so on.

This fear and worry is one of the biggest drains on our energy. To help, we need to look at the situations in our life and pay attention to our behavior.

Let us look at an easy example. You want to go out with your friends and you are worried about your spouse's reaction. First, does he or she have the right to tell you what to do? No, they don't. Do they have the right to ask that you be faithful to the marriage in all ways? Yes, they do. However, as long as you honor your responsibilities and agreements in your relationships, no one has the right to tell you what to do. If an agreement that you made with your spouse doesn't work for you, renegotiate that agreement instead of hiding your behavior with secrets and manipulation. Short-term, facing your behavior is hard, but long-term you will have a better life.

Standing in your power without the fear of getting in trouble means that you are not hiding your true self. People do not have to agree with you for the light of your essence to shine.

If respect isn't enough for smooth sailing in our relationships, then a deeper level of healing needs to take place. Usually, when respect isn't enough, it means that there is unresolved pain that needs to be worked through. Everyone believes in forgiveness, but few people realize that true forgiveness is a process that happens in stages and that emotional wisdom and divine perspective are essential.

It's hard to have real forgiveness without understanding the reason for your soul to have co-created the situation. This reason is sometimes personal or sometimes global. It can have something to do with our soul's history, or we could have participated out of love for someone else's lessons. Experiences can help us get ready for what's ahead, and the knowledge we acquire can be used for an upcoming event or person.

How do we know we need to forgive someone? The answer is simple. If you keep revisiting a situation in your mind, then you have unresolved issues that almost always boil down to either forgiving others, ourselves, or both. If we are in denial about forgiving someone, the universe will let us know by bringing the person we have issues with up in everyday conversations. Processing any emotional issue takes time, and it can be layer by layer. What that means is, we may have dealt with parts of the situation, but there are deeper, unconscious ones yet to process.

To set ourselves free from subtle intrusions on our happiness, forgiveness is necessary. It is something we do for ourselves first and others second.

Forgiveness

Step One: forgiveness is Intention.

It is time to make a choice and set yourself free from old pain or old memories renting space in your consciousness, taking up time and energy. Give yourself permission to focus on the intention of healing, which makes room in your life for new opportunities that provide a return on the mental and emotional energy you invest.

Step Two: assess the situation.

Without dwelling on the past, write down the memories, feelings, beliefs, perceptions, and people involved with the pain you are holding onto in a journal. This is necessary for self-awareness and wisdom.

Step Three: everyone's perception and motivation.

After you have given yourself time to honor your feelings, without justification or judgment, go over the experience again and put yourself in the other person's shoes. It is important to remember here that you are not justifying or validating the other person. Looking deeper offers insight into another's pain and emotional motivation for his or her behavior. Practitioner facilitation can be helpful in the process when we are unwilling or unable to see all the influencing factors offering objectivity and clarity. This information should also be written down to reference later if needed. Steps two and three can take several hours, days, or even years. Sometimes we are not ready to let go of pain because it still serves us. To forgive is to let go of pain and the need for validation from the person who contributed to the painful experience. This is easier said than done. One last thing in this section; it is sometimes difficult to allow ourselves to feel someone else's pain when we are in pain because of that person. Pain is pain, and it is okay to acknowledge it and the things people do because of it. Everyone has done something negative and hurtful out of pain.

Step Four: time.

Past experiences and the emotional clutter associated with them influence the way we respond to people in the moment, the choices we make, and how we feel resulting in a particular mindset, which in-turn creates our day-to-day reality and what we attract to us. We respond to others based on perceptions that are created from our experiences. This response is so natural, so instinctive, the conscious mind isn't alerted to the negativity we are creating for ourselves. The impact on our life is profound. This step takes the longest, and the information unfolds as we are forced to deal with different situations. This process takes time.

Step Five: change your mindset–change your life.

We sit down and make an agreement with ourselves. We decide we are going to change our mind. Sounds simple doesn't it? The ego and its connection to a certain pain or principle often makes it challenging. We must take a step back and reflect on the past situation from a broader perspective. The questions that need to be answered are: "Why did I co-create this situation or how can I turn it into something with a positive purpose? What are the gifts of awareness the experience has given me? What are the golden nuggets of wisdom I can claim and use to empower myself?" "What did the experience teach me about myself, life, my needs, my values, and my truth?" These questions may take time to answer, but it's worth the time-investment; without this information, we cannot move on. Life is complicated and nobody promised it would be easy, but learning to value peace and happiness greater than we value revenge, validation, or holding a grudge is life-changing.

Step Six: what do you really want?

This stage requires us to ask, "What do we want to create in our interactions or relationships with other people?" Most likely, our old pain has altered the way we see present situations and, of course, we respond accordingly. The old response will create more of the same and even more reason to be angry, insecure, stressed, or anxious. The key to achieving our desired outcomes is to alter any behaviors or lack of behaviors brought on by fear. Put simply, if we're taking action or choosing words motivated by fear, insecurity, or anger, then it's time for a change.

Most people require assistance when coming up with a plan of action, and after this is done, the passage of time and the outcomes will demonstrate what works and what does not. An action plan is about learning who you want to be in difficult situations and developing tools that support that desire. The tools can include productive communication when we are angry, stress release techniques to create more patience, learning how to communicate honestly and directly with respect, and so on and so on. Action plans may have to be changed or updated until the desired outcome takes place. If needed, consider seeking guidance from a professional.

Step Seven: communication.

The seventh step is using healthy, emotional communication and social skills. It may be essential to deal with the other person. If that isn't possible, writing a letter addressed to the person, and later burning it while saying a healing prayer, is helpful. Sometimes, small healing ceremonies are very beneficial and supportive in transforming old energy. Saying a prayer, lighting candles, and calling in God/Goddess to help, is powerful and can offer resolution when none is attainable through traditional methods.

Step Eight:

We need to focus on action plans until they are brought to completion, continuing to update it or change it as necessary. As we develop new response patterns to life, our reality will change and create better relationships with others. It is at this stage that some people regress backwards and let their minds dwell on the past. This usually happens while they are half asleep in bed, while they are driving, or anytime the mind is idle. When the mind does this, it uses up precious energy on past events and has less to offer the present moment or day. This is a waste of energy and can cause emotional imbalance.

Dwelling on the past is usually caused by repressed anger or unresolved feelings. It is crucial to recall what we seek, remain dedicated to that delightful conclusion, and pick contentment over the ego's attachment to the past. To reach our goals, we must remain mindful of the bigger picture, accept the lessons we are destined to learn, and never forget our heartfelt longing for joy. Over time, if we continue to nurture our positive intentions, the positive energy accumulates, becoming stronger than the negative, resulting in happy changes.

Even though these feelings may be subtle, and we may wonder if it is worth the effort. The impact on our relationships is real. We don't want to leave pieces of ourselves along life's path and feel hollow the further we go. It is important to go back and pick up those pieces of our heart, our essence, so that we may reclaim who we are and what we want. Only when we do this will we be able to fulfill our destiny and make a positive contribution to the world, which is something that we all should take responsibility for.

We are not in trouble. We can forgive ourselves and others, and we can stand in our power. It is our birthright to be happy; to love and be loved.

*FACE YOUR FEARS
TAKE BACK YOUR
POWER
AND BE WHO YOU ARE
MEANT TO BE"*

Parable Six
Journal Entry

"Moving On,"

 I have spent a lot of time thinking about lunch with Terri. It was bothering me so much that I scheduled a healing session. The practitioner talked about standing in my power and so on, but if I found that too difficult, then it can be an indication I have unresolved emotional issues from my past related to my personal power. She said the anger or emotional issues are created from past experiences/memories, and it's the past that contains the needed wisdom for healing and forgiveness, especially for myself, sometimes for just feeling what I was feeling. The entire conversation was a little confusing for me.

She said that I need to shine a light on my emotional shadows by facing them and acknowledging their presence. If I do this, I get the gift of myself back and will have full access to my Divinity. She said that I need to heal the old energy to make room for the higher vibrations of my being.

She also said the emotional shadows would tell me one thing: I am afraid, and I need to identify the fear that is covered up by the anger. She suggested I begin the healing process by communicating with the fear. Oh great, just what I want to do. Talk to myself about my anger and fear.

As I'm writing, I remember the dominant theme of my childhood. I was constantly trying to get approval. To get approval, I had to earn it, and I had to earn it in the way the parent wanted it to be. Unfortunately, because I was a child, I made mistakes. But there were many times when I didn't make mistakes and it still wasn't enough. They were so consumed by their own suffering and difficulties that they could not look beyond themselves.

I know they did their best, but I am struggling as an adult. I didn't get Terri's approval, and it is really bothering me. Whether or not I like it, I am unconsciously seeking peer approval to the point that I modify my words and behavior.

I have a lot of unexpressed emotional hurt, and I think I need to come to terms with my childhood and how love was expressed to me. It wasn't enough for me. I feel guilty about that and yet angry about it as well. I need to forgive my parents and myself, but first I need to acknowledge the pain that I am holding from those experiences. Wow, this is going to take a lot of work. My practitioner said to write it all down, give it time, and the emotional experiences that need to be processed or looked at will come with little effort. I just need to listen.

One thing I know for sure; It is an emotional burden I didn't realize I was carrying until Terri triggered me and I felt a combination of angry and insecurity.

I know my being, my gifts, my true self are enough now, as an adult, but I still get angry when someone challenges me. I still go into defense patterns that were born out of a disappointed child that was tired of being hurt. I have used these defense patterns to manage conflict or stress in my life, but they are not helping me achieve my goals.

I want to feel peaceful with myself, regardless of the outside world. I want to create healthy

*emotional and social skills, so I can navigate
conflict with wisdom. I want to be free of the
nagging voice inside my head that worries about
every paltry word or perception.*

*I will take some time and process memories and
pain that I am still holding on to. Then, I will
create something new!*

Chapter Six

Creating Happiness

Creating happiness is not as easy as one may assume, because our sensitivity is a key factor. We all have certain topics that cause us to be emotionally reactive, usually resulting in manipulation, anger, control, anxiety, and other insecure behavior patterns due to the way we perceive the situation before us. Therefore, choice is the changing factor in creating a new outlook and new mental/emotional programming.

Being rigid about the way we see a situation is a limitation. It goes with black and white thinking and is very narrow in its scope of reality. Life is complicated, people are complicated, and things are rarely simple, especially in relationships. If we want to bring about contentment, we must be prepared to modify the way we look at hard times. It's helpful to become more fluid, less rigid, and learn how to trust the path along with the Divine angels that guide and support us.

Anger contains nuggets of self-awareness and wisdom, so use it for this purpose. Wisdom attained through honest assessment of anger can answer important questions, giving us insight about who we are and what kind of life we want to create. Then, when we are in a difficult situation, such as an argument, we use the information to create progressive resolution and positive change by communicating our intentions, which represent our needs. This is the only way to be real and to be emotionally safe at the same time. Why is this so? Because when we are honest about our intentions, we do not have a hidden agenda. The other person has to respond to our truth and, therefore, change his or her response to us. Truth is a powerful force all by itself, dissolving the need to be protective.

Our emotional shadows, our fears, do not transform until we take action and change; the ability to change the way we see our reality and ourselves. To change our minds, we absolutely need to take responsibility for co-creating our negative experiences. Taking responsibility doesn't mean we agree with or justify another person's behavior. It means that we own our part, our history, and our fears. Note, in the scope of things that happen, such as a natural disaster, is part of living on a planet floating in a vast universe. It isn't personal, even though it feels like it when our house is destroyed.

With every wise decision, we raise the energy of our consciousness, and that has a positive impact on our life. How do we know we are making the right choices? Trust your instincts and only make the choice available in the moment that feels peaceful rather than easy. Often, we try to make choices without all the information and at the wrong time. Divine timing is a real thing. If in doubt, do nothing and wait. There is time; avoid rushing or chasing an outcome. We are gradually guided through trial and error, but this is far better than being stuck.

If we can trust just a little in the process and have faith that we are being guided, we can experience miracles. As we move into more evolved ways of living, we connect more and more to the high vibrations of joy and compassion. This influences the way we see ourselves and our world changes.

The tools of happiness are anger, wisdom, intuition, intention, choice, commitment, creativity, trust and faith. There is genuine power in being willing to change.

"THE LIGHT WITHIN ME CALLS TO THE LIGHT WITHIN YOU TO HELP MAKE THIS WORLD A BETTER PLACE."

Parable Seven
Journal Entry

"Replacing the Old with the New,"

"Breathe," my Angel, Ryan says to me. "When you are drowning in negative thoughts, bring your awareness to your breath. With each exhale, let go of the negative thought, and inhale a positive

thought or light. Do this repeatedly until your mind is focused on the present moment."

"But Ryan, as soon as I stop focusing my mind, it gradually drifts back to old, negative stuff like past conversations or memories. I mean, I don't think really hard about yelling at someone or anything. I just have a subtle, low hum of negative thoughts and feelings drifting in and out. Sometimes I don't even pay attention because the thoughts are so normal, and I have always been this way."

Ryan walks up to me in the visual meditation, puts his hand on my shoulder, "Seeker, you have not always been this way. You have forgotten who you really are and, in doing so, you have buried your gifts, your truth, and your brilliant illumination. I am just your guide, your friend, and if I could blow away this cloud of fear and confusion, I would. It is sad to see you in such pain. Pain that is self-inflicted is a brutal burden to bear. It is understandable while you are having a human experience, but if you could see yourself how I see you, you would be without such things as doubt."

Sighing, I sit down on the white bench. "I feel so stuck. I want to let go. I want to be happy. I want to believe in myself and I want to believe in love. I just don't know how to get there. I don't know the "how" and that bothers me more than anything."

Ryan sits down beside me, and I can see the loving support in his eyes. "How, is the human question that must be answered, and I know it is difficult, but nobody can answer it for you. The truth - the answer is different for everyone. What works for you won't work for someone else. All I may do is give you a few pointers, which you will think are too simple. You must have faith in the process that your own soul designed especially for you. And because you design it, only you have the answers you seek."

"To help maintain clarity and wisdom, refrain from becoming overly tired! When you are tired, you drift into negativity, so self care is number one and most important. The next pointer is also simple, but just as important, many people don't do it enough, and that is, you must be quiet with your own thoughts each day, which creates a reflective-peaceful mind. This means no book, no TV, no hobby, no doing - just being. This is very difficult for most humans because when they are alone, they want to busy themselves to feel comfortable in the quiet."

Leaning back on the bench, he continues, "It would only take 15 or so minutes each day. Energy that is not yours is constantly bombarding you, making this very important. Because of that, your mental and emotional energies can get cluttered. Taking a little time each day just to be in your own energy helps keep you centered." With a grin on his face, he says, "And don't ya think you have enough of your own energy to keep you busy, anyway?"

"Yeah, yeah, so is that all you got, Mr. Wise Holy One?"

He stands up, bows at the waist, "Oh thank you very much for the title, now you lowly human get on your knees and pay your penance." Then suddenly before I can respond, he's on his knees, begging, "Please forgive me, oh please for such arrogance," Batting his eyes at me and with a smirk he says, "I am your humble servant, my great human." Laughing hysterically, he sits back down on the bench and sighs.

"What was that all about?"
"Why are you worried?"

I just stare at him and he just sits smiling back, ever so peaceful and then finally says, "I was just playing with your greatest fear is all."

"And what would that be?".

"It is the fear of being too great or not being great enough."

"You see, humans know they are special deep down inside. It isn't your darkness you fear because you live with it each day, while most of your light is hidden from you. Your greatest fear is letting go of your old judgments and believing in your light. Not because you don't know it's there; you feel your light when you are quiet and when you express the energy of love. It is the fear of making a mistake by embracing your light fully and claiming your birthright as a piece of Goddess/God. Humans fear the responsibility of the light. You would be required to take full responsibility for everything you feel, think, create, and do."

"If you are wrong, and your Divine light is just a flicker in the shadows, then you are arrogant and sinning. If you are right, your life would change and you would shine brightly and others might judge. You would feel vulnerable or exposed.

Either way, your thinking process puts you in a corner. You sabotage your own progress."

"Well then, so what you're saying is I am screwed, and I am doing it to myself."

"Sort of. You have the key and you can unlock the door anytime, but you need to know how to find the door."

"But how do I find it?"

"I will leave you with one more hint for now. The layers of fear and judgment around the ego need to be shed, not the ego itself. The ego has one purpose, and that is to respect and honor the individual. It is your fear that twists the ego's energy. '

"While it's true, you reach your greatest potential when you are beyond the ego in spiritual form. You can't reach your greatest human potential without an evolved ego. It is impossible to create positive human relationships without honoring individual needs, and the ego represents those needs."

"Every need leads to one place, love. All people need to be love; to give love, and to receive love. As the ego sheds the layers of fear that surround it by changing destructive relationship patterns, the human balances and the evolved ego changes and merges with its Divinity. The individual achieves complete integration between the higher and lower selves."

"Individuality is still there, but there is no fear of lack or of union. You are then all things - all energies—all pieces of yourself at once and your 'intention/will' replaces the function of the ego, so you can decide who you want to be without limitation."

"We are all one, and yet, we have the power to individually create. What a wonderful gift."

Ryan turns to leave and I yell, "Wait!"

He enfolds me with the energy of compassion and, smiling, he says, "You don't have to know how; it will just happen when the time comes and you have unlocked your door of doubt. Trust yourself, it is you who has created this path, and it

*is you who has the map that leads to the door. Let
the **path and its guidance** unfold gradually and
have faith in the process."*

*Waving goodbye, he turns and disappears into
white light.*

Chapter Seven

Keep your eyes forward

'Keep your eyes forward, otherwise you might fall', so the saying goes. Once we have reviewed our lives up to this point, we need to look towards the future. It's important that we don't rush through our history lesson, however, but to dwell is not useful.

We hear a lot about being positive, focusing our energy, etc., but we already know about that. Let's talk about contentment. How do we create a life that is relaxed, enjoyable, and loving without feelings of lack, doubt, stress, and struggle? Positive thoughts do very little if we still hang on to our negative feelings and doubts.

If we become emotionally invested in someone else's opinion, it can bring up insecurities or fears. For example, what if they are right and you are just fooling yourself and you are wrong? For us to stay in our center, we need to stop making it about right and wrong and trust our instincts. Even if our instincts lead us towards a difficult situation, it was ours to go through and it was ours to learn from. Outside opinion is only helpful for one reason: information.

Information helps us assess our life path and helps us determine how it serves our growth. Even if our family and friends don't agree, the choice is still ours. Our instincts help guide us in making decisions that are the best for us. Everyone learns differently, and everyone needs to give him or herself permission to go through life in the way that works for the self.

As our life path helps us unfold our potential, it is helpful to remember who we want to be, and here is how to begin.

Many spiritual books can leave the reader feeling well informed, but practical application is often elusive. These kinds of books are so idealistic that they leave one important ingredient out of the equation - the ego. The spiritual books out there concentrate on helping us let go of the ego. In doing so, they give us the sense that our ego, our individuality, our humanity, is less than our spiritual counterpart.

Our human experience is miniscule and fleeting in comparison to our eternity, which is what I think might be causing this impression. However, our soul grows through our ego and through our humanity. All of us come from the same source and our human experience allows our soul to develop and experience individual creativity. How do we merge our individuality and our Divinity?

We need to remember that there is no way that we will grow without being honest about our nature and addressing the ego. The ego connects to our emotions and fears. Emotional triggers are spontaneous and much harder to predict or control. The ego is imprinted by the inner-child and is created by our emotional responses and interpretations of an experience. If we incarnated as a fully formed adult, the ego would be in harmony with our Divine wisdom, but instead, we incarnate as helpless babies with parents who are dealing with their own emotional flaws and the patterns start from there. Our emotional triggers are based on the past and the belief system we created. Please note here that our beliefs are not facts or even truths. They are perceptions.

The key, the first step, but not the only, to being who you really are and reaching your personal, spiritual potential, is to ask "Why?" For example, "Why did you say that? Why did you respond to that person in that way?" These questions are critical for our personal healing. Questions like these facilitate self-awareness. We cannot heal what we are not aware of existing.

Let's explore what this process would look like in the real world. The first example will lead the person to a positive answer. The second will lead the individual to a negative answer. What we do with the information determines our happiness.

The first is an example of positive self-value.

"Why did you say that?"
"He made me angry." "Why?" "Because he hurt my feelings with his judgment, and I don't agree with his statements."
"Why do you care about his statements?"
"I don't care,"
"Then why are you angry?"
"He is wrong."
"Why is he wrong?" "He doesn't really know me and doesn't have any right to judge me."
"Again, why do you care about his opinion?"
"I don't care, I'm just angry."
"Why?"
"I feel hurt."
"Why?"
"My feelings were not considered, and he was emotionally cold."

"Why do you want your feelings to be considered?"

"I matter. I have feelings. I have value!"

The purpose is to decide the best action to take. Did you dishonor yourself by repressing the genuine pain, or did you allow another to dishonor you by not speaking your truth?" If the answer is "no," then don't waste anymore energy on the situation. If the answer is "Yes," then you need to create an action plan. This action plan may include changing your behavior or future responses in similar situations or it may actually mean processing it further with the person who represents the emotional trigger for you. Remember, the goal isn't agreement, but mutual respect.

Let's look at the second example with a negative outcome.

"Why did you say that?"

"I wanted to share info and help."

"Why?"

"Because I know what I am talking about and it could help him."

"Why is that important?"

"I want to help people."

"Why?"

"I value helping other people."

"Why?"

"I feel good when I help people."

"Why?"

"I feel needed, productive."

"Why do you need to be needed?"
"Because it's who I am."
"Why does that define you?"
"I need to feel needed, to feel love."
"Why?"
"If I'm not needed, then I don't have any value."
"Why do you need to give to have value?"
"If I don't feel valued, I don't feel good enough and I won't be happy."

In this example, the individual is allowing fear and insecurity about self value to create negative energy in his or her relationships. If too much time passes, this person will eventually feel tired, resentful, and angry.

Our ego is part of our self-value and our value is part of our Divinity, so we cannot separate ourselves from our individual needs. It is important to process the needs and feelings of the individual in relationships and while creating harmony with the emotional needs of others.

Being idealistic is wonderful, but by itself it will not help us decide who cooks, who pays the bills, or how two people process their anger and work out agreements of behavior. To create a compromise between two different people with different needs and belief systems, we need to create respect. How do we create respect? We create it by balancing the needs of the individual with the needs of others. This may seem like an impossible ideal. The truth is, "need" is easy to fulfill. The hard part is going through the layers of anger that cover up the real emotional needs of the individual. The best question we can ask ourselves is why?

Creating a positive, loving future and keeping our eyes forward is the balance between the wisdom gathered from our past and the actions that we take in the present. If we want to truly be a loving person and leave a positive impression on this world, we need to be happy in our own being. Our ego, our feelings, our Divinity, all have value. Once we respect ourselves, we can appreciate the worth of other people, and that is known as mutual respect.

"THERE ARE MANY DIFFERENT KINDS OF INTELLIGENCE, BUT ONLY ONE TRUE WISDOM: COMPASSION."

Parable Eight
Journal Entry

"Actions"

"Hi, Ryan."

"Good morning, Seeker, I am glad you have come to our meeting place today. We have much to give you."

"Good, because I am still very confused."

He smiles. "Come sit by the river with me."

I walk towards him and we sit down on a wood bench facing the river. For a few minutes, we say nothing. Instead, we enjoy watching the sun glitter off of the water as it flows downstream from right to left. The river is only about fifteen feet across, small enough to be peaceful and large enough to lift your spirits with its song. I let go of my mental confusion and relax, and I feel myself open and my breath expands into my lower belly. I feel quiet.

I can also feel Ryan waiting patiently, allowing me this time to let go of stress and center my Spirit. After some time passes, he gently touches my shoulder. "Are you ready, Seeker?" I nod and turn my body towards him.

He smiles again as if he knows some secret. "I want to share more information with you concerning the human ego."

"Good, because I understood what we discussed last time, but I am having a hard time using the information in my daily life, and I am still fumbling."

He pauses, looks me in the eye and says, "There are three important things to remember about the ego. First, the inner child in each human creates the ego. The ego is already established by the time you become an adult. Therefore, the needs of the ego are often childlike. Now, let me clarify this before I go on. That isn't to say the needs are immature, we will always be children of Goddess/God. I'm trying to explain that the needs are pure, almost innocent. The second is the ego is both passive and aggressive. It will be a lot easier for you to see the aggressive or verbal side of your ego. The passive side is almost unconscious. It will take time to become aware of this side of the ego, but you will find its expression in your emotional voice inside your mind. It is the part of the ego that plans and quietly goes about its business. When your body isn't relaxed while talking, it's because it's your ego that's doing the talking.

"You see, the ego is never peaceful. It is always doing, always protecting, defending, and always attaining something in the material or spiritual world. Your body will tighten, your breath will become shallow, and your face will change. When this happens, you are speaking through your ego."

"Remember, as you walk your life path, your truth evolves, and so does your ego. The last attachment for the ego is to your individuality, and the ego fears losing it. The ego is afraid that if it lets go, then it will dissolve and no longer be. This is not true. Your individuality doesn't exist in the ego, but in your will or intentional desire. What you will yourself to be is what you are. You do not need the ego to be an individual. Its only purpose, which will always remain as long as you are

human, is to evolve your Spirit. It is through the ego that you learn about yourself and life."

"So, how do I begin?"

"Good question! You probably won't like my answer because it isn't all wrapped up in a bow for you. The answer is different for everyone. There are many different spiritual paths that facilitate the evolution of the ego. People connect to the path that is comfortable for their belief system."

I cross my arms over my chest and look out over the river with an exhausted look of dismay on my face.

He laughs. "Okay, I will ask you a question, and your answer to this question will help you begin. Here is the question. If all of your worries were taken care of; no money, relationship or career issues, everything was in perfect balance, what would you wish for?"

I look at him cautiously. "No worries, no issues?"

"That's right, it's all taken care of; what would you wish for?"

"Hmm…" I think for a minute. "It can be anything?"

"Anything,"

"Well, I would wish to experience more magic and enchantment in my life."

"Okay, now the second part of the question is, what kind of personality characteristics would a person who wished for magic and enchantment have to have?"

"Well, it would be a peaceful person. One who loved serenity, quiet, and small joys. That kind of person would enjoy nature, books, meditation, spiritual connection, and perhaps need lots of alone time."

"Yes." He smiles. "You have just described a piece of your core essence. It's a piece of your true nature the ego tries to protect and express. The things you do each day with your family and career are also parts of who you are. Those parts of your life are the areas that you choose to experience for growth, but the core piece of your essence never changes. It is always there, no matter what situation you are in."

He Continues, "It is self-denial of this core essence that creates fear, struggle, and pain." Standing up, he says, "Your first step would be to create a lifestyle that incorporated your true essence so that you may be happy in your own being. When you create happiness for yourself, the ego doesn't need to fight for it and you will begin to speak and live from your heart."

I see a large sphere of light appear and I know this means the meeting is over and it's time for him to go.

"Relax, let yourself absorb the information. Everything is in perfect balance. You will get there, just have focused faith and remember who you really are." He waves and disappears into the light. I think to myself, 'what the hell is **focused faith**?'

Chapter Eight

"Balance between Focused Faith, Compassion and Action,"

The further we walk down our spiritual paths, the greater understanding we have of the universe's energy patterns, also known as life-force energy. For example, as we look inward, we discover needs, dreams, and goals tucked away in our spirit. We think that if we could just find the right job, the right lover, the right amount of money, then we have succeeded in life. The first attempt to live a better life is to think about what we don't like, heal or change it, and then create action plans to create something else. Granted, this is powerful and is an important step in pursuing a better life. Eventually, however, it will get us only so far.

Soon after some progress and a few years of deep growth, we max out the action plan's potential because, by itself, it only has so much power.

We begin to feel stagnant and when this happens; we get a little frustrated. The frustration comes from knowing too much. We begin to understand the function of our ego. We understand what needs to be healed and what needs to be changed in ourselves. We know what we want with more clarity. Yet, as we look around, we still see struggle in our relationships. We still see struggle with money, and we still see our ego expressing itself in negative ways. We also still experience fear of change, fear of lack, and fear of being ourselves or expressing our true nature. So, what do we do?

We have gained enough insight and wisdom to understand how the universe functions and the law of attraction. Put simply, what we focus on or nurture accumulates energy, grows, and we attract the resulting manifestation of our consistent intention. We have come far enough to know that there is more to life than going to work, paying bills, having some fun, and being in relationships. We can sense it. Deep within, we can feel a desire, a knowing of a deeper truth, a spiritual and powerful presence waiting for us within. Some label this presence as Goddess/God. Some say it is the Spirit or the Soul. But these are just words and though these words may have meaning, it doesn't tell us how it feels to live within this presence and live within this world at the same time.

How do we progress from here? Many teachers would say, "Change your reality." These words are not enough. Life flows fast, like a flooded river. Energy is limited; Time is limited, and we only have so much of ourselves to share. If left unchecked, life is overwhelming, causing stress and struggle. Understanding how we contribute to and create self-imposed stress is important.

There are many things to consider about life and the universe that affect our spiritual-life path.

Number one: the ego. Much of the ego is unconscious. Understanding when and how we use it takes years, but this knowledge is vital for self-mastery.

Number two: we are all one. Everyone understands this concept, but few realize its power. The connection we have with each other creates the global reality. Every choice we make as individuals either contributes positive or negative energy to others and the planet.

More people are considering how their choices affect the quality of life on the planet and also in their personal relationships. We are evolving and changing, creating an influx of transformative energy. It feels like we can barely keep up with our to-do lists and obligations. Humanity is living at a faster rate more than ever before and let's not forget, the almost 8 billion people living on the same planet. Wow! That is a magnitude of energy bouncing back and forth from person to person.

Number three: we need to remember that we are spiritually growing at a very fast pace; faster than any other time on the planet. We are under a lot of mental and emotional pressure to heal our issues because they are so acute. It is almost impossible to repress anything right now. The issue will either come out in physical illness, or relationship and money struggles. Issues that usually took several years to become annoyingly uncomfortable are becoming acutely miserable in only a few years. This is both true for our personal life and global life with other cultures. It is hard to feel balanced when we are constantly growing and changing.

Number four: spiritual contracts. Some people call them Karma or some people call them destiny. It doesn't matter what we label it; we are here on this planet for each other as well as ourselves.

There are many energy patterns that have been created in Earth's reality that humans can only transform because we are the cause. We can only transform energy by experiencing it in the physical or 3-D world and then by making better choices. This gradually transforms fear-based energy patterns as the positive energy accumulates over time, manifesting healthier dynamics. This is the universal law of cause and effect.

We are also here to heal old relationship patterns that are not love based with the people around us. This means that we can be doing really well and then out of nowhere an issue comes up in our relationships, and then we have to heal some forgotten mess we started years ago.

Of course, this is only the tip of the iceberg of things to consider when we are trying to be balanced. Life is complicated, and it isn't all about us all the time. We are here together, and it is together that we will heal and grow.

We need tools, ideas, and concepts. That is how our brain functions. As we evolve, we need less and less of the tools and more and more of being in our truth. However, getting from point A to point B is a little tricky. We are limited by what we know to be real and to expand our reality; we need to expand what we know. This is only accomplished through experience.

We hear it all the time; "I could be happy and peaceful if I could just get such-and-such. If I had the right relationship or enough money, for example, then I wouldn't be as worried. I would have more energy to pursue other things." This statement is so wrong in so many ways and we even know it is wrong, yet we hear ourselves and others say it all the time. Even when we have everything we need to be happy, we still worry. We still procrastinate on things that we know we need to take action on. We still repress our emotional issues, we still ignore our passions and our gifts, and we still have struggle in our lives.

Here we are towards the end of this chapter, and finally we find a nugget of hope. It is a glimmer of light in the shadows of our consciousness. We wait for it. We sense it coming to the surface and we hope that it points us in some direction so that we can stop going in circles. We pause... and then we put together what we have learned so far. We wove this wisdom into one square. On this square we see the words *Focused Faith, Compassion and Action.* We realize we must blend all three into perfect balance to take the next step on our path.

FOCUSED FAITH is the understanding of the larger spiritual and universal influences in our lives; that what we are experiencing in this world is divinely guided. We are here to grow, to learn, to heal, and to share our light. Nothing will change or stop this process, even if we resist change. Staying focused on the things we actually have control over–mainly speaking of one's mind-set, choices, and attitude, and having faith in the rest resolving in its own time exactly the way it needs too.

Focused Faith is also about focusing on our divine passion and walking towards it; trusting that as long as we follow our heart, the rest will be taken care of. Our divine passion is always present; it is a matter of removing all the layers of doubt and procrastination that cover it up. What we need to remember is that our natural gifts and our divine passion are complimentary.

For example, my gift is communication, teaching, and dissolving fear with truth. I was a born tinker of ideas, and I need to express my thoughts. However, it took me a long time to connect this gift with my divine passion because I don't necessarily feel passionate about writing, but I do feel passionate about my thoughts and ideas. I have learned that my life flows easier if I write because it is a divine expression of the passion within me. It doesn't matter where my life leads me as long as I fulfill my soul's purpose and use my natural gifts. Remove the layers of doubt covering your true nature and, with focused faith, pursue a path that uses your gifts, allowing your goodness to flow.

COMPASSION transforms fear. It is both soft and hard. Our truth floats in a bubble of compassion. When we are worried and afraid, we need to connect to the compassion within us. We need to sit with it quietly and breathe it into our consciousness. It is here, in this quiet compassion, that we hear the wisdom of the Divine guiding us to the right choice for the moment and for the situation, which, of course, may change as time passes. We can take any conflict or struggle in our lives, sit with compassion, and we will get the information we need to heal the situation or, at the very least, contribute positive energy towards a future solution. Hearing the divine, wise voice within takes self-control and time. A person can do this by lighting a candle, sitting quietly, meditating, and asking self, "If I set aside my anxiety/anger, focus on what I actually have control over, let go of the rest, what advice can I hear from within?" We will not progress and attain peace without incorporating the vibration of compassion in our being.

One more thought about compassion, its vibration is higher truth or love, not right or wrong or even good or bad. Sometimes the most compassionate thing we can do for someone is to let him or her struggle till they fall. Some people will not change in any other way. Sometimes the most compassionate thing we can do is to be silent, and sometimes the most compassionate thing we can do is speak up for ourselves and others. How do we know? If we are speaking from the ego, we are not speaking with compassion, but with an agenda. If we are speaking from our personal truth — without attachment — we feel peaceful inside and we are in the vibration of compassion.

ACTION is still very important. When we have achieved a level of growth and healing, our mind is clear and our goodness flows through our gifts. It's important to take action and use the gifts we have been given, even if the perfect relationship or money isn't available exactly as we would like. Life is designed to make sure we stay in our own lane; what we can control has limits and therefore, life will present us with situations that are difficult or stressful. These situations give the soul an opportunity to grow in ways that otherwise would be impossible.

If we don't take action and use our gifts, we will create lack in all areas of our life and we won't be truly happy or satisfied. We need to use our gifts and have faith in their power to create a life path of happiness and well-being. All of us need to have faith in our own gifts and goodness and trust where they lead. This is not goal motivated, but rather it's a need or yearnings of the heart. For example, if our natural gift is joy, to those around us, and if our lifestyle isn't joyful, then we can't fulfill our soul's purpose. This form of self-denial creates depression. Taking action in this way is more about creating a lifestyle that supports your true nature and gifts. Career choices have very little to do with it as long as the environment or job allows someone to share his or her goodness, gifts, and individuality.

Minor changes and small steps create an increase in positive energy. *With Focused Faith, we trust ourselves and Spirit. With Compassion, we gain wisdom and guidance. With Action, we take back our power regardless of struggle, and with intention, all three come together to create the perfect, divine path for our life.*

"WE LOOK DOWN ON OUR WOVEN SQUARE OF WISDOM AND TAKE OUR FIRST STEP TO THE NEW FUTURE."

Parable Nine
Journal Entry

"Divinity"

With my intention, I stepped into the
visualization and Ryan was already there, lounging
on the bench by the river. His angel wings
shimmered in the sunlight, producing a rainbow of
soft pastel colors. I noticed right away that he was
in one of his high-energy moods. "Good morning,

Seeker! I see you are being proactive by taking the time to meditate, which is essential on the spiritual journey."

Smiling, I sit down beside him and listen to the melody of the river. He patiently waits while I take a few minutes to relax and center myself. Turning to him, I asked, "How did you know I was going to meditate this morning?"

"That question is a great way to begin our discussion today. We are going to talk about the Divine and exactly what it is and what it does."

"To answer your question, I knew you were going to meditate this morning because, based upon present choices, Spirit can predict the immediate future. We cannot predict the long-range future because the future changes as you change your choices in the present moment. We can only see long range potentials, but the outcomes can be altered and they often are. In

addition, as your Angel guide, I am connected to your Spirit, consciousness, mindset, and the potential choices you might make based on your needs, emotions, and thoughts. Put simply, I can feel or read the energy broadcasting from your intention and Spirit, at any time or any place."

Continuing, he says, "Before every human is born into a body, there are several meetings. In these meetings, your soul's life purpose is discussed along with who your Angel guides and Guardian Angels are going to be. Most of the time, the human soul has worked with these guides before and there is much love, friendship, and respect for each other. Sometimes there is a role reversal and the Soul that was in human form switches places and becomes the Angel guide. Then the Angel guide becomes a human."

"You see, we can be of service to each other and to the planet in several ways. Some choose to be in

human form, some choose to be guides, and others want to do both."

"I have chosen to experience both and so have you, Seeker. However, during this go around, I am your guide and you are the one in human form."

This information gives me pause, and I need some time to comprehend it. Looking at him, I say, "How can this be true? I don't remember being anything before being me."

He smiles, "You are Divine and you are whatever you will yourself to be. A spiritual, Divine life-force energy created you, and that same power is yours to access and use for creating."

"If I was an Angel guide before, how come I can't remember?"

"If you were to remember everything, Seeker, that information would influence your choices *and you would sabotage your potential learning process.”*

“Oh.”

“The Divinity's primary concern is to be, to express, and to create because that is what Goddess/God is, a creator. That Goddess/God spark within us gives us the need to create no matter what. We would be bored with life if we couldn't create something with the Divine life-force within each of us. The Divinity's main purpose is to create and experience. It holds no judgment or fear towards anything. It looks at every experience as an opportunity to feel and to learn. We want these experiences to evolve so that we may expand our awareness of existence.”

“Okay, why do we then have so much doubt?”

“I'm so glad you asked that question. Self-doubt is the biggest obstacle for a human. You doubt

everything. You doubt your words, you doubt whether you should say what you really feel, you doubt your choices, and you doubt your spiritual value."

Ryan leans back on the bench, and stretches out his legs. "The answer I have for you has two parts. The first part is that self-doubt is part of the divine plan of life. Your journey through self-doubt teaches you lessons that you cannot learn any other way."

Seeing the confusion on my face, he expands the answer. "Let's take parenthood, for example. Many people can tell you what to expect, what to do and so on, but unless you actually go through parenthood yourself, you really don't fully understand what it means. By going through the experience, you learn things that cannot be taught through communication."

"This is true for most of life's lessons. The human needs to experience the issues first hand to gain the emotional understanding he or she needs to grow. Therefore, self-doubt, which is fear, is the teacher, the tester. The process of working with and moving through self-doubt that allows the soul to attain true wisdom.

"Now, moving on to the second part of my answer, humans give too much of their power to self-doubt. You use it as an excuse not to move forward."

"If self-doubt is so intertwined with the human path, what can I do to work with it better?"

"Another good question; and this is the last one I will answer for today. The first step is to alter how you view the choices available to you. Most humans try to make decisions based on the right or wrong method. If they are not sure what

choice to make, it immobilizes them and they don't make any choice. This long process wastes so much time and creates struggle. Instead, look at each choice in a more open way. First, take back your power and give yourself a way out if you don't like something. Give yourself permission to say no, wait for more information, or change your mind if you don't like the result of a path taken. If you have an idea to do something, but are not sure if it's for you, then get more information and take a small step towards that idea. For example, if you want to be a massage therapist, the first few steps to take are to get regular massages, as well as interview massage therapists and teachers. The next step you may try is attending a free seminar, and so on."

"Okay, Ryan, I did all of that and I was still unsure? It is a lot of money to spend."

"Well, remember there is value or wisdom in every experience, and do not worry so much about the money. Money is energy, just like everything else. It comes and goes and it means nothing upon your death. The wisdom and love that you attained during the lifetime is what counts. Money is never a good reason to decide whether or not to do something. Take the necessary time to attract the extra funds, but gradually pursue something if it feels important, even if you don't understand why."

"Look at each experience the way your Divinity looks at life. You will learn something about yourself and life no matter what decision you make. Making this learning a part of your journey can help you progress, so it's never a bad decision or a waste of time. This is the true meaning of spiritual success."

"It is so much easier and so much harder than you can imagine. Easier because spiritual success means living fully; exactly the way you want to, and

harder because you must take back your power from self-doubt and face your fears."

He stands up and says, "But if you can do this, you will leave this planet without regret and your Spirit will be full of joy. **This is the true meaning of success."**

A white light appears; he steps into it and vanishes.

I am left pondering over my thoughts as I look at the river.

Chapter Nine

"Surrender"

We need to mention just a few more things about the ego and about our Divinity. It is important for the ego to surrender in order to access our Divinity fully. Note, to surrender doesn't mean to be without. Rather, it means to let go control over things that we cannot control anyway, and to let go of attachment to outcomes. There is only one way to accomplish this, and it is extremely difficult to do: live a balanced, satisfying, emotionally wise, spiritual life. Most people consider surrendering attachment to outcomes to be weakness or loss, but in this situation, it is a position of great strength and wisdom. We learn constructive, effective control over self by understanding what we can and cannot control, and in doing so, we learn the skill of surrendering to the outcome as it is guided by the Divine. In other words, trust.

We accomplish true peace if the ego surrenders to the divine path by giving up the need to protect us from pain for it's part of life no matter what. The outcome of a situation is in alignment with each person's highest good long-term, even if we do not understand it. If one person was given control over others, then he or she would be responsible for another's growth and evolution, opening the door to dependency and pain. We are not meant to have control over others, for it would interfere with individual free-will, learning, creativity, and growth.

Love can be difficult for the ego. It's more comfortable in protection mode since it doesn't like change or challenges. It usually expresses this protection with anger, anxiety, passive/aggressive behavior, sarcasm, manipulation of information or perceptions, and control. Somehow along the way, the ego has twisted its purpose of honoring and respecting individual value or free-will. In truth, we don't need to protect ourselves, prove our value, or ask permission.

We need to return to who we are - to what we are: Divine life-force energy. This is not something that needs protecting. Truth is truth, and the Divine has unquestionable value, and since we are divine, our very existence establishes value. The Divine does not need the ego to protect or to prove its worth. These are human fears created by our environment and incarnating as a helpless child with little power versus incarnating with a fully formed mind and in control over our environment. This disadvantage forms the shadow side of the ego, which gives us plenty of opportunities to learn and grow. Image how different our lives would be if we incarnated in the physical, as adults with fully developed minds and personal power. It's just a thought.

Surrendering the ego, or control, or attachment feels uncomfortable, but long-term it's worth it. The first step is to trust that we are children of Goddess/God and nothing changes that. Every person has his or her own journey and lessons. The soul has a plan. Who are we to question another's highest good? Kindness, self-control, love, and making the right or wise choice at any given time is a far more productive use of our personal power and free-will. Notice, I didn't say the good or easy choice. Often, making the right choice, given what we actually have control over and what we do not in a situation, isn't easy. It takes love, wisdom, and patience.

The next step is to remember that the Angels surround us always and that our emotional needs will always be honored by the Divine, even if we can't create a way to do that in our relationships or situation. There is peace in knowing that we always have somewhere to go when nobody else is available. This awareness is the key to redirecting the ego's energy.

Why does the ego energy need to be redirected in the first place? Because fear motivates the ego's protection patterns and it's our motivation that creates our life. There are three forms of fear: **Anger–Control–and Pride**. All three are lower vibrations and they create struggle or unnecessary pain.

Allowing the ego to surrender to the Divinity within or another way of saying it, our higher-self within is very difficult to accomplish in everyday relationship situations. There is hope, however. We are more than our ego, our soul, and our Divinity. We are also a human consciousness, also known as the spirit. It is the human part of us that governs free-will. Either fear/ego can motivate us or love/wisdom, but that doesn't change the fact that free will resides in the human part of us. Choice is the only true power we have, and it's the only thing we have control over. What are you going to spend your precious time on today?

Earth is the free will zone. We learn from experiencing the results of our choices. As we gain wisdom, we make better choices. The Soul evolves and experiences the gift of creativity through the human. Let me explain further. The Soul vibration carries our life purpose, destiny and karma. The human part of us uses free will to create, learn and accomplish the Soul's agenda.

If the human can learn from its experiences, and not allow the ego to take over, it can create miracles. How fast the human learns and attains wisdom is determined by the individual's ability to change and grow. It's also known as surrendering to the process or path and accepting what needs to be done.

Some people become rigid in their energy and they take the long road. They are black and white thinkers; it's either positive or negative. Life isn't that simple. Their lives usually have numerous struggles because of the need to control others and protect themselves from pain. People like this complain about the same thing repeatedly, resisting the truth. (We often know what needs to be done, but we simply don't like the answer.) They spend their time repeating the same relationship patterns, choices, and behaviors over and over again.

As we can see, the human part of us has the actual power in this reality. Therefore, if we desire to have more peace and express our Divinity in this world, we don't have to be victimized by our own ego. We don't have to let it rule and sabotage our happiness and productive use of personal power or free-will.

To surrender the ego, means to have trust in the higher power within us, and to let go of the need to release anger immediately, which is very addictive;

self-control is challenging when we are angry. We need to come to the understanding that nobody outside of ourselves has the power to tell us what is right for us. It is a position of personal truth without the need to prove it. This is neutrality and power.

This understanding reduces the ego's defense systems, motivating us to focus on creating the life we want to experience. We can begin by writing down the things we value and why. Then incorporate this value system into the daily schedule. For instance, an individual might need alone time to replenish his or her energy. Then scheduling alone time each day or each week would be important to well-being, creating balanced mental and emotional energies.

We will know when we are being motivated by fear, when the ego expresses anger, control, or pride. It is the darker side of these three that teaches us about our compassion.

We are most afraid of our flaws or imperfections being exposed. We are afraid of our limitations and we are afraid of our power. As we change how we relate to our flaws or lower vibrations with grace and kindness, we learn about compassion.

The vibration of compassion is truth and love in their highest form. When we surrender and let go of attachment, we nurture the divine within. Wisdom becomes attainable, giving us the guidance we need at the right time. We might not like the answer, but we can trust it. Love flows freely through higher truth and compassion. It will show us what actions we need to take and when.

The inner power known as self-acceptance and self-reliance means to stand in one's value system - one's Divinity - without seeking approval and without being needy. It means peace, and peace is the pathway to the Divine. We mentally and emotionally realize that there is power in our flaws. They have purpose. They exist for a reason: to help us create what works and let go of what doesn't. They help us identify our truth and our inner light.

Above is what we need to do, but how do we do it? The following process is just a suggestion; a place to start. Walking the path in our own way is important.

Fear is the main reason we create struggle, so that is where we need to start. How do we process our fear in a healthy way?

- **Write down what we truly value in life and why we value it. Basically, we assess what we need and love to be happy and well.**

- We then need to create action plans from the list above so that we may have a lifestyle that expresses our values.

- Next is the understanding that we are most afraid and protective when our value system is threatened or judged.

- We also need to recognize that when we are expressing Anger–Control–and Pride, we are in ego/protection mode. This means that something has triggered a fear or insecurity.

- Identify the fear as soon as possible. To know what fear something has triggered, we ask, "Why are we feeling this way? What are we afraid of losing or not getting presently or long-term?" Answering these questions will help you determine which element of your value system is being challenged.

Lastly, ask self, "What is this situation trying to teach me about myself and about life? The response will lead you toward what modifications must be made in your life's outlook and approach to living.

Implementing the action plans and making needed changes in our behavior is the moment of power. It is the moment of mental and emotional transformation.

By being proactive, transforming our negative patterns and focusing on what we value, we manifest a happy life experience. When we feel insecure, the ego goes into old patterns of protection, and protection has solved nothing.

Our fears and value system are connected. What we value most is what we fear losing. If we let anger, control, and pride rule our life, peace and happiness will be out of reach.

Go through the process of self-awareness and acceptance and let your soul, which carries the spark of the Divine, take care of the rest.

"TRUE WISDOM IS ACCEPTING WHAT IS AND UTILIZING ITS FULL POTENTIAL."

Parable Ten
Journal Entry

"Disapproval"

I am full of frustration! I can't stop seeking approval in tiny, little ways. It's a subconscious habit effecting almost every decision I make. This pattern haunts me. I don't know how to stop the emotional responses." Suddenly feeling tired, I stop my pacing and sit down on the bench beside Ryan.

Ryan pats my shoulder. "It takes time. At least you have achieved enough self-awareness to observe your behavior. Most people don't admit their insecurities to themselves."

"But I need more help! I know that I know better, but I can't seem to make it happen emotionally. How do I change this pattern? Please give me some kind of clue, something, anything."

"First, I have two questions for you. When do you notice yourself seeking approval most often and when do you notice yourself defending your reasoning about something?"

"Well, pausing to think a minute before I reply. I feel it in very subtle ways most of the time. It can be about how I do something or how I look. Those don't bother me as much as feeling disapproval from others about how I live my life and what I value. It really bothers me if I make

someone angry at me because I disappointed them."

"Go on, Seeker, keep going."

"Hmm.. I notice it is mostly with my spouse or with my parents. Sometimes what I like or want to do, they don't agree with and they judge it as less than. It feels like they think I am messing up."

"You are doing very well, Seeker. This is where you need to go. What do you feel during these kinds of situations?"

"I get angry and I justify my behavior and my feelings. I also try to defend my position by explaining my needs. When this happens, I feel a sense of judgment and disapproval. This makes me even more angry of course, and I either shut down or express my anger verbally."

"Either way, I am still upset after the situation is over and I feel drained by the experience. The worst part is the feelings stay with me. Help me, Ryan. What do I do? How do I stop this cycle?"

"Take a deep breath in, Seeker, and relax. Your mind needs to absorb new information first before you can translate your awareness into an experience and emotional feeling."

I take a deep breath and let it out. *"Okay, I am ready. What do I need to know?"*

"Now, the information I am presenting doesn't necessarily go in order. It is for you to take in as a whole package."

"To start with, you need to accept the sides of yourself that others don't approve of. Find the reason or positive purpose in your so-called flaws. When you find yourself feeling angry in

an approval situation, stop–pause–think–feel–
instead of continuing to talk. Give yourself time.
This may mean you need to change the subject,
leave the room, or pause before you respond.
Giving yourself time will allow you to use
discernment with your words and take the action
that is best for you."

"Moving on to more information, remember
that you wouldn't be happy if you lived your life
for others. So even if you had their approval,
leading the life they thought you should, and
doing the things that they find valuable, you still
wouldn't be happy. Next, and probably the most
important, is that everyone's soul has a purpose.
Sometimes the spiritual contracts and purpose
for a soul aren't always normal or easy to
understand. When you accept that your choices,
your needs, and your life are an expression of
your soul's purpose, it seems silly to compare
yourself to others."

"How are you doing so far, Seeker?"

"Not too bad. Is there more?"

"Well, of course there is more!" He smiles.

*"It is a mistake to take judgment too seriously
because people, including yourself, will judge
from their own perception and value system,
which will always differ from yours. People
think that their beliefs and values are the best, so
they will judge yours automatically without even
realizing it. The question is, 'is this true for
you?' If it's not, let it go."*

*"I will let you in on a little secret that might
help a lot. Every child seeks approval from his or
her parents and later on from spouses, but not in
the way you might think. The actual need for
approval has nothing to do with lifestyle choices.
It comes from the need to be seen as a valuable,
worthy individual - just because you are alive. It*

is feeling worthy of love; feeling as if you are enough, just as you are. This also translates to your relationship with Goddess/God and that is where you really seek it."

"Can you tell me more about what you just said?"

"Sure. As a human, you are in an interesting situation. On one hand, from childhood, you can feel your Divinity and instinctually know you have value. On the other hand, life doesn't always make you feel that way, which creates doubt and the shadow side of the ego or lower-self. This duality motivates you to seek confirmation of your self-value and at the same time, creates resentment when you don't get it."

"So, what you're saying is that I know on some level that I don't need peer approval, yet because I might have doubts, I seek it unconsciously anyway, which puts me in a

163

*double bind. I will never get peer approval
100% of the time and I will resent it when
someone suggests that my ideas and feelings
don't have value. Is that what you mean,
Ryan?"*

*"Almost," he says. "Your need for complete
unconditional love and approval is instinctual.
What you are seeking in the human world can
only be attained in the Spiritual world. To solve
this dilemma, it is helpful to develop positive
relationships (usually with friends and family),
where you can feel accepted most of the time.
During the times that you need more comfort,
you can turn to Goddess/God. It is in that
relationship where you are truly known and still
truly loved and valued."*

*"But, what will I do the rest of the time when
I feel triggered in my relationships?"*

*"Pause–think–feel and give yourself time.
Remember that it is a waste of your energy to try*

to convince someone that you are right from your perspective."

"If you try to convince someone that you are right, you are not honoring their feelings and are treating them exactly the way they are treating you. Instead, try to nurture respect in your relationships, not agreement." Continuing, he says, "When experience hurt feelings, go within to your soul, to your angel guides, and to Goddess/God and seek council. We will comfort and guide you when you doubt yourself. Please take the time to cultivate stillness, creating the emotional and mental space needed to hear the higher-self and the Divine within and without. Negative emotional energy is draining and does not contribute positive life-force energy to your life."

"What you need to realize, Seeker, is that most of the time the people around you are trying to get their needs met by proving their

value, including your parents, spouse, boss, etc.
They, too, are trying their best with insecurities.
**So the next time you feel judged, remember
where it is coming from.**"

With a smile on his face, Ryan stands up,
waves goodbye, and walks into the white light. I
sit there for a few moments absorbing the
information, and then I open my eyes.

Chapter Ten

"Control"

Control has been discussed in previous chapters, but it's such a common personality trait, it merits further exploration. Most people do not even admit to themselves that they are controlling. There are many different expressions of control and everyone has at least a few. Control and approval are closely linked. We fear that what we want will be withheld. Our unconscious reasoning or shadow-side suggests that the best way to get approval and still get what we want is through control and manipulation; specifically manipulation of information guiding another's perception in the wanted direction, which creates assumptions and associations that do not accurately show or explain the complete story.

Control is passive, aggressive, subtle, in your face, and easy. Everyone exhibits behaviors of control on and off throughout his or her lifetime. Control has its place and, when appropriately used, is positive, such as tempering one's anger. It can also be destructive and is probably the leading cause of relationship failure.

Control's close cousin is rigid. Being in control usually means being rigid in one's thinking and feeling. Another word for being rigid is closed. To be closed is to resist change, and to resist change is to resist life.

The areas in our life we try to control are our home or situational environment, our emotional exposure or honesty, our beliefs, other people, and the outside world. If we are exhibiting one or all of these behaviors, we are inadvertently controlling or manipulating the people around us through our words and actions.

The subject of control is important and powerful because it affects all areas of our life, especially in our relationships. Control also flows both ways. We are the one in control, and sometimes, we feel controlled by others.

The subject of control can trigger many people because most of us justify our reasoning for the control and others don't want to acknowledge their control issues because they would have to look within themselves and what motivates them.

If we could just find a way to get what we want through communication instead of control or manipulation, our relationships would be healthier, reducing stress and improving well-being. However, childhood teaches us that if we state what we want, we usually won't get it. As adults, we still carry those memories. We have learned from experience that manipulation and control will get us what we want instead of asking.

There are many problems with this behavior, but the most important is that control will only give us what we want in the short-term.

The most subtle form of control is through action or inaction. There are few words exchanged on the exact agenda or subject being controlled because the person expressing controlling behavior is using tactics that are meant to distract. The information and intention are hidden from others. Life has taught us that people are highly motivated to create what they want. There is nothing wrong with people getting what they want. It becomes an issue when what we want prevents someone else from getting what they want or manipulating another's free-will or perception.

The forms of subtle or passive control are **manipulation, inaction, hidden motivations, stubborn thinking, immaturity, neediness, guilt, environmental control, dependency, and pushing one's will on another through laziness, or refusing to change.**

Subtle control turns into obvious or aggressive control when the controlling person is challenged verbally. The forms of aggressive control are **anger, aggression, whining, mental head games, verbal defense patterns, closing off emotionally to resist change or to punish the other person, and domination**. These kinds of patterns usually result in a verbal fight where one or both people end up walking away without resolution.

In these kinds of relationships, we are usually being controlled and also being the one who is controlling. We always draw our equal in relationships, so if we are being controlled, we are also controlling in some form or we have lessons to learn around personal power and boundaries.

Let's explore victimhood: "how can someone who is needy and who is a victim be controlling?" (Note: I am not discussing abuse in this example. I am referring to a person who whines about everything continuously looking for the negative in all situations.) Victimhood is a powerful form of passive control because the victim doesn't have to take responsibility for him or herself. They don't have to heal, change, or stand on their own two feet. They can blame all their struggles on everyone else. Victimhood allows them to justify their behavior and life without working hard to change.

Believe it or not, it's sometimes harder to look within and heal than it is to be a victim. Sometimes victimhood comes from a place of ignorance and not resistance. In these situations, outside help may be required, however even if the victim doesn't know a different way of living, they still have instincts. Goddess/God gave us natural instincts to let us know when we need to change regardless of our emotional and mental evolution. This means that regardless of how we have become a victim in our lives, we are still responsible for co-creating the situation and changing it.

Victimhood is a chapter all by itself and needs more explanation than provided right here, but I wanted us to understand that control isn't a black-and-white issue. Control is grey, complicated, and common.

So, how do we create win–win relationship patterns without control? We have already covered several of the steps and tools in this book. To refresh our memory, I will list the highlights.

- **Becoming self-aware and learning about what we need to be happy in this world is very important.**

- **We also need to look at our emotional baggage and heal it.**

- **We need to change attitudes, beliefs, and patterns that no longer work for us.**

- **We stop comparing our unique needs and gifts with others, to prove our goodness, to have outside approval, and we give up the need to be right. We recognize that true wisdom lies in making the right decision for the situation.**

- **We become aware of the larger picture and realize every**

person is on a life journey with its own set of lessons, gifts, and agenda. We might not know why things are as they are, but we can trust in the divine purpose of the learning process. We can trust the path.

The larger picture reminds us that there are reasons for everything. Our experiences may have elements of good or bad energy, but taken in their true wholeness, are made of several different energies that all come from love. The Angels said to me one time when I was trying to fully understand something that I had experienced, **"Love is the life-force of life, and it is love that will heal you."**

The above summarizes the things we can do to become less controlling, but let us address the control directly. Foremost, if we carry fear in our being, we control on some level and in some situations. To heal control directly, we need to face our fears as they come up. The most common fears that motivate control are: fear of losing what we have such as our family, our house, our money, etc. Fear of not being good enough, fear of not being accepted, fear of not being loved in the way we want to be, fear of change, fear of emotional exposure, fear of our free-will or freedom being taken away, fear of pain, and fear of being unhappy.

The first thing that may come to mind is that these are damn good reasons to be in control, and I won't disagree with that assessment. Unfortunately, we know fear creates struggle and we know that control motivated by fear doesn't support a happy life with loving relationships. Control may give us a feeling of protection and keep us from experiencing acute emotional pain, but the price we pay for our illusion is that we live a painful life long-term, regardless. The pain might not be as acute, but we quietly carry it with us in our hearts. This negative energy limits our love, our happiness, and our potential.

To heal this, be honest. Facing our fears when others trigger them transforms our control patterns through osmosis. It may be acutely painful to face our fear and change, but the pain will only last a few hours or days. That is better than the rest of our lives.

Our first step is to be honest about what we need, and give up manipulation and control to get it. Closing ourselves off and refusing to change creates a backlash of pain as time passes. Instead, I would encourage us to get what we want through communication, giving self permission rather than looking for agreement from others, and respect. We are not children anymore, being victimized by our parent's belief system and issues. We can choose to value ourselves without outside approval, and we can ask for what we want. We can learn how to create win–win agreements in our relationships without control. If we can't, we can move on because you know what? We are all grown up now!

"THE INNER-CHILD HOLDS THE SECRETS, THE GIFTS, AND THE WISDOM OF THE SOUL."

Parable Eleven
Journal Entry

"The Inner-Child,"

"Ryan!!!" Where are you? It's not working!" I sit down in exasperation on the bench beside the river. I fold my arms over my chest and look out at the water. The sun is reflecting like glitter along the gentle current,

and it soothes me.

I am very frustrated. I have listened, and I have tried to put into practice what I have learned; yet, I still feel like I am repeating the same stuff except in different packages. The same issues, along with the same emotions, are still getting triggered. I want to be free of this old baggage.

"Ryan! Where are you?" Instantly, a white light encompasses the bench I'm sitting on. I hear wings as the wind swirls around me. The white light enfolds me, filling me with a deep feeling of peace. I can feel the wind blowing away negative energy as I am filled with healing energy.

The white light pulls shifts to the bench beside me and I watch as Ryan materializes within the light. On the other side of me, two more large white orbs appear, and as I watch, I see White Lake appear, along with my guardian angel.

Ryan speaks first. "Ah... Seeker, do not despair. We are with you. You are never forsaken. We hear every call, every prayer, and we are always present, helping in any way that we can. You are never alone with any burden, worry, or issue. We are with you always!"

Mary, my guardian angel, walks forwards and sits down beside me on the bench. She takes my hand. "Seeker, life is too precious for you to get lost in the illusions of your fear."

My other spirit guide, White Lake, pounds the end of his staff on the ground and a medium size boulder appears. With a satisfied smile, he walks around it and sits down, joining the rest of us.

"You know, Seeker, he says, you are your own worst enemy."

This, of course, immediately angers. "What do you mean, I am my own worst enemy? I'm doing the best I can. I am following the rules. I am trying to make conscious decisions. I am taking action and working on the plan. My own worst enemy, huh! What?!"

White Lake chuckles and looks at Ryan. "Do you want to answer the question?"

Ryan laughs. "Nah, it's your turn."

White Lake sighs just a little and looks at me while Mary continues to hold my hand so that she can help my energy stay focused.

"Let's take you to the next level, Seeker, and the best way to do that is to talk about your

inner-child."

"White Lake, if you're going to tell me that all of my feelings come from my inner-child and that the inner-child motivates my decisions, I already know that."

He chuckles yet again, "Well, that is a good place to start, but since you have that part covered, we will take it further. I have a question for you. Do you know what it feels like when your inner-child is making your daily choices?"

"Hmm..it feels like normal. I mean, something comes up and I feel a certain way about it and, based on those feelings, I make a choice. Is that what you mean?"

"Exactly. Now, do you believe this is the best way to live?"

"I guess so. I don't know any other way and it seems pretty healthy."

"If you continue to live in that way, Seeker, you will always return to this state of frustration."

"But White Lake, I am working hard on making better choices, facing my fear, and taking responsibility for my experiences and what I create. How much more can I do? I thought the inner-child was an important part of our development and that this part of us needs to be honored and loved."

"Of course your inner-child is honored and loved, Seeker. I am suggesting you take the understanding of the role of your inner-child further."

"The inner-child's feelings are both fear and love based, therefore, the inner-child is the motivation for your love and kindness, as well as

your control and anger issues."

"Now pay attention; this part is very important. The inner-child's job is to show you what you need to be happy. It is the adult's job to take the information it learns from the inner-child and make the best decisions that honor those needs. Most humans, however, let the inner-child rule their everyday thoughts and choices."

"The adult is a by- product of the inner-child. It is the grown aspect of the inner-child. The adult has gathered wisdom and, with that wisdom, it can heal the inner-child. In return, the inner-child feels valued and loved, sharing with the adult its joy and wisdom beyond the physical world. To take this further, when the inner-child feels loved and valued, the door to its essence unlocks, creating a conscious connection to the soul.

"The trick," as he shakes his finger at me, "is that the inner-child must first feel worthy of the

Soul's Divinity. The only way it can feel worthy is through the adult who becomes the parent, protector, and friend."

"So what does this mean in the real world?"

"The real world; do you hear this? White Lake asks the group. Seeker thinks the real world is <u>real</u>." He slaps his knee and laughs. "Yeah, yeah, I am so funny; make fun of the dumb human."

"We are not laughing at you, Seeker. We are using joy to open your mind, to break down your mental barriers. You're going to think my answers are too simple for your questions." Suddenly, he turns to Mary. "Maybe you can answer theses questions for Seeker in such a way as to bypass the mental barriers."

I shift my attention to Mary, who turns towards me and smiles. "The answer is something that isn't only understood, but felt." She places her hand on

*my heart chakra, filling me with a wonderful
feeling.*

*I close my eyes, enjoying the sensations; feeling
the tension leave my body. With my eyes closed, I
can hear Mary speak in my mind. "Life is love and
love is value. To love is to place value on
something or someone. Love and value don't
require you to like or agree. It means honor and
peace. All of your answers are here in your heart
chakra. Activate the wisdom in your heart, in your
spirit, by turning to it in all situations. Act with
integrity and be in your Divinity."*

*Mary drops her hands from my heart chakra and
continues, "Listen to your inner-child's needs,
concerns, and fears, but do not let this part of you
justify negative patterns. Find better ways to get
what you want. Find better ways to honor yourself
and the people around you."*

"Ask your inner-child to help you create a value system that works with your emotional needs and joys. From there, let the adult and the Soul work together to create happiness. If you let go of the need to protect and control, you realize that the best kind of happiness and existence comes from being abundant in your energy, your dreams, your love, and kindness."

"What about my struggle, worry, and frustration?"

She smiles. "Seeker," she says," you need to listen. Your Soul has the wisdom, power, and tools to transform any struggle to success. The inner-child must be an active participant in this relationship, but all three parts of you work together to face any circumstances with success. There isn't anything that comes your way that you can't succeed at. We are telling you how to go about it. Love the inner-child by listening to its needs and in return the inner-child will give you the keys to your happiness."

"I have one more question. How do I know what my inner-child is saying?"

"Oh, that's the easy part, Seeker. The inner-child speaks most of the time through the ego, which is the constant voice in your head. The one that's angry, that worries, that complains. If you listen to this voice, you will find the needs of the inner-child. When you hear this voice, don't ignore it. Take but a moment and ask yourself these questions: What is my real concern in this situation? How does this person or situation make me feel? What am I afraid of? Underneath the emotions are the needs and values. If you know what you value, then you know exactly what choice to make in all situations. With this clarity, you have wisdom."

"Okay, do you have any more suggestions that will help me out?"

"Yes," Ryan pipes up. "Take some time to get to know your inner-child consciously. It would be helpful to participate in some inner-child meditations. Ask this part of yourself once a week, what he or she would like to do, and schedule that activity in your weekly schedule."

"What will this do?"

"It will show that **you value your inner-child enough to set aside time for him or her each week. It shows your inner-child love improving self-worth**. When you see the value in yourself, you will see the value in others. This will bring you wisdom that will help you create harmony in your relationships."

My heart swells with gratitude and with it, peace. I feel more peaceful in this moment than I have in weeks. Looking at these loving beings, I say, "Thank you, all of you. I will follow your advice."

Chapter Eleven

"Okay - The Negative People,"

Okay. We understand the inner-child and its importance in our spiritual development and in our relationships. We also understand that if we take some time to listen to each other, and be willing to communicate, most things can either be healed or accepted. How do we heal a situation when the other person doesn't cooperate or isn't interested in healing or changing?

We all know people in our lives that we feel are too negative to deal with, yet sometimes we find ourselves in circumstances that involve them, anyway. The solution to this very common problem isn't simple or easy. It is usually possible and can be done on an individual basis, if a person is committed to taking responsibility for his or her own choices and resources.

To put it in simple terms, what we have learned so far is that we need to honor the Divine in others and ourselves. We have discussed some details on how to go about that in relationships and so on, but it is really hard to work with people we **don't want** to deal with. How do we stay in our integrity and see the Divine in others when we think they aren't living their life at the same level as we are?

In the following, I am going to list some suggestions and tools that may bring clarity to life's unpleasant struggles. I will offer real-life examples for deeper understanding.

TOOLS AND SUGGESTIONS

- *Be at peace with yourself and know who you are and what you need to be happy and loving.*

It sounds simple, I know, but knowing yourself is the foundation you stand on. If you don't know what you need or what you value, you will be walked on.

- ***Handle the situation according to your integrity and value system.***

It isn't wise to adapt yourself to someone else's values and sacrifice your own. It will only create pain. There must be a balance that works out for all involved.

- ***It is good to know how far you are willing to go and what the other person is capable of doing.***

In other words, remember at all times whom you are dealing with and know what they are capable of. Don't ask someone for something they lack the ability or inclination to give.

- ***Speak up for yourself regardless of the fear and struggle.***

Most people don't speak up because they are afraid of losing something or are afraid of the conflict that may result. Do it anyway when the timing feels right. If you live with the resentment, it turns into bitterness. Creating financial and emotional security gives a person options and the ability to walk away if needed.

- ***Ask yourself if this is an important issue, meaning does it affect the quality of your life and your relationship with the person?***

If the answer is "Yes," then take action. If the answer is "No," then pick your battles wisely and let the small stuff go.

- ***Karma. If you are caught up in a conflict with another person, most of the time, but not all, it results from karma. Now, this isn't necessarily karma with this particular soul. It can be a karmic pattern that someone is helping you transform, and they, too, have the opportunity to transform their own in the situation.***

Take responsibility for co-creating the situation. You are NOT a victim; you are an adult with personal power. Remember, karma can be with that person or it can be universal. The difference is that if you have karma with the person, your souls agreed to the experience for mutual growth. If karma is universal like war, for example, then it is karma that involves all of us and your soul agreed to work with the energy for the greater good of all. We all have personal and global reasons for being here.

- ***Stay away from power struggles.***

This is the hardest thing to remember. As soon as you go into who is right and who is wrong, control and protection patterns, you have just created a power struggle. The result will be a verbal fight until one or both are tired, without a resolution. Remember, you do not have to prove the value of your needs to anyone; ever.

- ***Know when to walk away, let go, or change.***

If little to no progress is made, then you need a change of scenery. You may have to change a job, let the person go, or walk away.

- ***Ask for help.***

There are many times that a third party is very helpful in resolving conflicts between people. The third party, however, shouldn't know either of you personally and should be qualified to handle the issue.

- ***Do not lower your vibration to match the other person's energy. Stand in your integrity by***

remembering who you are.

We have heard the saying "Don't stoop to their level," but what that looks like in the real world, is that if a person sends you a nasty verbal arrow that attacks your character, don't address the arrow, which is simply a distraction, but instead, deal directly with the behavior. Stick to the facts, the truth, and disregard the rest because if they can make you angry, they can distract you. If you are distracted, they can hide their fears and emotions. It's an old trick used since the beginning of time. Don't fall for it.

- ### *What does this conflict and/ or person represent for me?*

This is an important question to answer because the answer tells you if you can heal the issue internally, or if the other person needs to be addressed to heal the issue. To solve a problem, we usually need to look both internally and externally by directly addressing the person. If you are working with a negative co-worker and they trigger your insecurities, for example, you better find out what your lessons are in the situation as soon as possible in order to evolve the situation.

- ### *Let go of the outcome.*

The outcome is always divinely guided and in alignment with the highest good for all. If you experience an unfavorable outcome, it's for a reason. The reason is always to help guide you along your life path, providing learning and wisdom. What might look negative today will change over time as you gain greater understanding and self-awareness.

- ### *We are mirrors for each other.*

Everyone has heard this concept before, but it's often misunderstood. When I say the word mirror, it is more than the person mirroring your emotional issues to you. Half of the time is doesn't mean that at all. When someone is mirroring your energy, the role they play facilitates your learning process about yourself. They can push you and help you understand how powerful you truly are.

Sometimes the person is there to provide you the opportunity to heal an issue and therefore, the mirror aspect displays your growth rather than a characteristic trait. The last thought to mention about the mirror function is its ability to operate in opposites. We mirror the other side of the issue to each other, which, when looked at in depth, is saying the exact same thing.

For example, one person spends a lot of money, and the other saves. You see these two kinds of people in relationships all the time. The spender teaches the saver how to enjoy life at the moment because you might not make it to retirement. The saver teaches the spender how security can also be enjoyable. Together they bring balance and they are mirroring the same need/truth to each other, even though they are on the opposite sides. They both value happiness, just in different ways.

When we have a conflict with another person, it can often trigger several issues at the same time. It is wise to focus on the situation at hand and leave unrelated feelings out of it.

Still, the most difficult part of working with negative energy is feeling secure with your actions. Often, we ask ourselves if we are being un-spiritual, controlling, projecting our issues, etc. We fear that if we are experiencing negative situations, then we must be missing some spiritual truth, and if we could only figure out the secret, then we would move beyond these petty struggles with others.

Ahh, well…isn't that the trap we fall into?

There is the assumption that spiritual wisdom means peace. It is more accurate to say that spiritual wisdom means the ability to handle negativity while still maintaining a peaceful heart. It doesn't mean a life without negative people, though some may disagree, instead it means we change our attitude about negativity. People are just people. Sometimes they are good and sometimes they are bad, but it changes nothing. We are still one global family.

The reason behind this logic is that in their extremes, both positive and negative energies mirror each other. They both are goal oriented and self-righteous. The ego influences anything that involves goal attainment.

The individual is wise enough to hold the vibration of peace in his or her heart and wise enough to work with negative people or situations to help those who need it. However, working in the negative energy with a peaceful heart doesn't mean we just send light to the situation. That is a huge misconception in the metaphysical community.

"How do we have the best of both worlds and still work with negative people?"

The Bodhisattva (a spiritual person who has moved beyond fear) would say we have to give up the wanting of anything, because he or she would know the truth; that if you surrender, then you get a glimpse of the awakened spiritual mind and the only thing left is to stop trying. I personally love this concept. It is a place beyond the ego. It is a very reasonable concept if you are not in any relationship and live on a mountaintop.

I am sure that it is possible even if you don't live on a mountaintop, but just a tad bit harder to create. Well, maybe a lot harder. Of course a Bodhisattva would say the ego and belief systems are getting in the way, and of course he would be right.

We are more than willing to go to Bodhisaville, but the path that leads us there is filled with opportunities to transform fear. We cannot ignore or repress our fear if it exists in our emotional and mental energy. It isn't something that can be taken from us because it is a piece of us. We need to transform it back to truth/love energy. The only way to transform human ego/fear is by learning from it and the experiences created by it. Negative people and situations reflect to us our issues like a mirror. The transformation occurs as you surrender to the experience and participate. To hide from or ignore conflict is to repress our fear, creating a lack in personal power.

So until we reach a point of not wanting anything and in doing so, have everything and we are without fear on any level, we can use the tools that are provided.

The following are some examples of how we may transform negative energy in everyday situations.

Okay, here is our "aha!" moment. In all conflict and struggle, the most important question to ask is, *"What would I do if I wasn't afraid?"* What would you do if you weren't afraid of losing your job, of being honest, of being un-spiritual, of gossip, of disapproval, of losing or succeeding? Now, this doesn't mean you need to take action right away. Most change occurs after thorough planning. Take action at the right time, in the right way, based on your individual needs and goals.

Keep this question in mind as you read the following examples and though these examples are inspired by real-life situations, the characters have been dramatized and the stories are fictional.

TOM CAT

You know the tomcat that likes to mark his territory in the way cats do. It can be so petty, but it can be so aggravating. Let me tell you about a situation that can fit into several scenarios.

Two neighbors—one property line: Neighbor number one, Mr. Tom Cat builds on his land and is very pleased with himself. He loves his new house, fulfilling his dream of retirement.

Neighbor number two is Mr. Enough. Now Mr. Enough is tired of getting the short end of the stick. He feels that if he treats those around him fairly, they will reciprocate. Unfortunately, Mr. Enough hasn't been that fortunate. Instead, he finds himself constantly dealing with people who don't match his value system.

Mr. Tom Cat isn't a bad man; he just goes about his business fulfilling his personal agenda, trying to create what he wants. He isn't too concerned about fair play unless he has to be fair to get what he wants. They call this Attitude of Entitlement. If Mr. Tom Cat isn't challenged and his bottom line for his personal survival isn't threatened, then he doesn't care. In his own mind, he can find an excuse to justify his behavior. From his point of view, he isn't doing anything wrong, so why should he change?

Mr. Tom Cat accidentally built a solid structure on Mr. Enough's property. Now Mr. Enough, believing in fair play, told Mr. Tom Cat that he would lease the five feet along the length of the property line without charge, if Mr. Tom Cat would put some trees on the property line for mutual privacy. At first, Mr. Tom Cat agreed and signed the contract. Then, after some time passed, Mr. Tom Cat decided he didn't want any trees along the property and sent a letter to Mr.

Enough saying that he would not cooperate.

Mr. Enough went to a lawyer and realized that if he decided to sell his property, it would cause problems with a sale and that if Mr. Tom Cat was left unchecked, he could grandfather the land, which would result in him getting Mr. Enough's property.

As you can see, by not cooperating, Mr. Tom Cat has nothing to lose. He doesn't have to tear down the structure on Mr. Enough's land, nor does he have to pay for trees, and he will end up with extra footage for himself if he waits Mr. Enough out and calls his bluff.

To get any action, Mr. Enough would have to spend money and push the issue. Money and energy that Mr. Tom Cat hopes he doesn't have. So when it comes to manipulation, Mr. Tom Cat is perfectly playing his cards. However, when it comes to fair play, he isn't.
So, Mr. Enough faces a dilemma. Is it petty of him to worry about 5 feet along the property line? Is this issue worth the extra money and energy to take it to court? Mr. Tom Cat is counting on Mr. Enough to walk away from the issue.

The mirror energy is Mr. Enough is teaching Mr. Tom Cat to live with integrity and fair play. Mr. Tom Cat is teaching Mr. Enough that he is entitled to what he owns. Together, they balance each other out. They both deserve to be happy and they both live next to each other and need to take into consideration the needs of the other.

What would Mr. Enough do if he weren't afraid of spending the money and taking the situation to court?

What would Mr. Tom Cat do if he wasn't afraid of losing money and wasn't afraid of change?

The result is that Mr. Enough, after giving Mr. Tom Cat one more opportunity to negotiate (fair play and all), takes him to court. A third party needs to get involved because Mr. Tom Cat doesn't want to take part. Mr. Enough could walk away, but it will eat at him and long-term, it affects the quality of his life.

To maintain his integrity, Mr. Enough will need to let go of the outcome. He follows the steps, takes back his power, fulfills his role and lets the highest good see to the outcome. This is key to being a spiritual person and still having to deal with life's negative surprises.

As Mr. Enough takes action, he transforms his fear of loss; as Mr. Tom Cat has to face the issue, he also transforms his fear of loss.
They both are worried about losing the same things: power, money, happiness, and free will.

Mr. Enough, who is spiritually aware, has to deal with Mr. Tom Cat, who is personally motivated. By working together in this negative situation, both men get the opportunity to grow. Mr. Enough heals old wounds through the present situation and Mr. Tom Cat heals old emotional protection patterns, while both men transform their fear.

The most important part of working with our own emotional fears is to let go of the outcome. We need to understand that our soul will take care of the details if we show up, surrender, and participate. We can trust the outcome of any situation has our well-being and growth in mind long-term. We don't know, what we don't know.

The following is the second example.

PASSIVE AND AGGRESSIVE

We will call these two characters Ms. Control and Ms. Positive.

Ms. Control insists things are her way, and she works with Ms. Positive, who insists on keeping the peace.

Ms. Positive is actually Ms. Control's boss, however she doesn't really emotionally own this position. Her spiritual value system encourages her to stay positive, give problems such as conflict over to God; that everything will work out in the long run. What she doesn't realize is that her spiritual purpose might be to actually confront Ms. Control about her behavior.

Confrontation terrifies Ms. Positive because she doesn't believe it solves anything; because it makes her feel things such as anger that she would rather not deal with.

Ms. Control doesn't really mind conflict as long as she wins. She is afraid that if she doesn't get things her way, then she will be unhappy. Her fear tells her that control and being right equal happiness. Granted, this is mostly subconscious on her part, but if she took a moment to analyze her behavior, she would have a hard time denying it.

Both women mirror the same thing to each other. Both are afraid of being unhappy. They hold on to their beliefs so strongly that they are blinded by them and cannot see another way. This is an example of black and white thinking.

The situation is, Ms. Control is pushing her agenda and telling Ms. Positive how to do her job. She is trying to take control of the business decisions and telling Ms. Positive, whom she thinks she should work with.

Ms. Positive is trying to keep the peace and is putting up with Ms. Control's interference. She believes that if she says a few things here and there, that Ms. Control will get the hint and change her behavior. Of course, she is sadly mistaken, and Ms. Control continues pushing her agenda. Ms. Positive is getting frustrated, but she tries to handle her anger by praying about the situation and asking the Angels to heal it.

It isn't until other people complain about Ms. Control's behavior that Ms. Positive realizes that sending light to the situation might not be enough.

Before we go on with the example, let us discuss the fears that are operating in this situation. Ms. Positive fears that anger equals negativity. She also fears owning her power and taking responsibility, which would translate into her communicating her emotions. To her, emotions are confusing and uncomfortable. She feels insecure about her leadership position and she doesn't want to make people angry who work for her. She desperately wants to uphold her positive, peacemaker image. To do that, she can't directly confront someone, in case they get angry.

Now Ms. Control has a similar fear as Ms. Positive. She is worried about looking weak and stupid. Her self-value comes from her being the most powerful and intelligent person in the room. She knows she is right and if she can prove it to others, she will be the leader she secretly hopes to be. She is also afraid of her unpopular emotions and tries to hide them by being controlling. Her greatest fear is that others won't see her value, so she pushes it on them.

Both women fear their emotions and both are seeking approval from outside of themselves.

Okay, back to the story. Ms. Control finally pushes Ms. Positive so far that a conflict manifests. It leaves both women blaming each other and parting ways. This throws both of them into a whirl of anger that brings their unconscious fears to the surface.

Ms. Positive's instinct is to smooth things over and to recover her peacemaker image to avoid disapproval.

Ms. Control responds by going out of her way to prove she is right and the better of the two. She aggressively protects her belief systems to convince others she is right and therefore, attempting to avoid disapproval.

It is interesting how both women are playing off of each other's insecurities and fear. They weren't healing the issues on their own, so their Souls agreed to work with each other for mutual growth.

Here, the Divine purpose wasn't being light and positive, but instead, it was learning about being honest with one's true feelings.

It helps to remember the Divine is always available for assistance. They guide and support us through life's challenges. It's interference for them to take the lessons away from us. It isn't in our highest good for them to wave a hand and make it disappear or suddenly make both people healthier.

Wisdom and healing are only attained through emotional awareness and transformation. Spirit can't do the work for us. We need to heal our own issues if we are going to grow. Sending it to the light isn't enough.

We pre-judge things so much that sometimes we are oblivious to the higher purpose. In this situation, it wasn't meant for the women to become friends. They were playing roles for each other that were divinely guided. The purpose wasn't to be without conflict, but to gather more wisdom and healing so that eventually, they both will get to a place without conflict. But that isn't today. They have more healing to do, and it is only the ego that would convince them otherwise.

This brings us to the next point. Often, it is the struggle in our lives that exposes the ego. Our external environment will inform us if our beliefs about being loving and spiritually advanced are true or not. The outside world holds us accountable with the facts of life.

We need to have a positive attitude when it comes to struggle. It is only through our attitude that we have a peaceful heart while we deal with life. Ms. Positive could use her positive attitude and face the conflict head on instead of hiding in fear. Having a positive attitude and embracing life's up and downs creates internal peace, and peace is happiness.

If both women had redirected their energy to being honest about their fears, the conflict would no longer have a purpose and they would dissolve it.

The next and final example shows a different approach to moving through life's struggle. The above examples are about taking some kind of action. The following describes a situation that requires an active person to be more passive without hiding.

CLASH OF THE TITIANS

Again, we will take the workplace as the setting because most of us can relate to that environment. The characters are called Mr. Leader and Ms. Loner.

The background of Mr. Leader is that he desperately wants to be respected. He tries really hard each day, proving his skills and why they are so helpful, but because he tries so hard to prove he is a leader, he comes up short. Therefore, when he talks with someone, he is selling himself. The conversations always reference his skills and opinions.

The background of Ms. Loner mirrors Mr. Leader. She doesn't know how to sell herself and prefers to be left alone. She finds herself constantly in leadership positions she doesn't want. Her skills and methods are in the same areas as Mr. Leader, but she has fundamental differences. Her approach and processes are different and she doesn't enjoy justifying them.

In truth, their methods are both productive; some people will be attracted to Mr. Leader and some to Ms. Loner. Since they both work in the same company, things tend to get a little sticky.

They are equals in their positions, neither being the boss of the other, but both working in the same department.

The situation is that Mr. Leader doesn't like the attention that Ms. Loner gets. He is noticing that several people were shoving Ms. Loner's skill and methods in his face. He doesn't enjoy having to fight for attention and respect.

Ms. Loner stands out even when she tries not to. Yet, she is compelled to be vocal rather than be silent on issues that come up at work. She doesn't like negative attention that comes with sharing her ideas with others and being active in the work community.

Mr. Leader is part of that negative attention she doesn't like. She hears him gossiping about her and telling others her methods are lacking. She puts herself into a pattern of proving her self-worth to others when confronted with Mr. Leader's opinion of her skills.

Ms. Loner wants to take the high road and has the attitude that there is enough room for everyone. She is right, of course, but Mr. Leader doesn't go away. He continues to feel threatened by her, yet if she were to confront him, his ego wouldn't admit to it. So what does she do? Does she confront him anyway? What does she say to the people who are bringing her the negative information, which feeds her fears?

The first thing that Ms. Loner asks of herself is, 'why was she in this situation?' She is spiritually aware enough to understand that she is a co-creator of her life experiences. As she thinks things through, she remembers her past.

She remembered a time when she was working for another company. She had the same experience with another co-worker that was very similar to Mr. Leader. She remembered how she became furious and confronted the co-worker; how she vocally tried to prove herself to everyone around her. She would argue her viewpoint, and in doing so, she noticed it didn't really make people understand her more. In fact, even though she presented a good argument, proved that her co-worker was the one out of balance, people turned away from her, anyway. This past experience was one of the reasons she avoided leadership positions.

The problem here is that Ms. Loner's life purpose is to be a leader. Her soul carries the vibration in this lifetime, so no matter what, she can't avoid the energy. Her first step is to accept this is part of her life's journey and not fear it so much. To deny her natural gifts will bring her depression, listlessness, and fatigue.

Leadership doesn't necessarily mean being in the public eye. It can mean a person who is an

212

*initiator of ideas behind the scenes in the
environment. Some people gather information
effortlessly, and it's their job to share it with
others. In the sharing of ideas, they find
themselves sought by their peers.*

*When Ms. Loner realized she was repeating
the same set of issues, she acted differently in the
hopes of avoiding another painful situation in
the future. After all, Mr. Leader was just being
himself and, by doing so, he was helping her
heal her fears.*

*Mr. Leader isn't spiritually aware, so the only
thing going on in his mind is to land on top. He
figures that if he can prove himself enough, his
authority will be unquestioned. In doing so, he
feels respected and intelligent. Even though he
isn't aware of it, Mr. Leader is on his own
healing path, dealing with the same insecurities
as Ms. Loner.*

*They both are afraid of being unworthy of a
leadership position. Both fear that they aren't
good or wise enough. They cope with these fears
in different ways, but they trigger each other
because they mirror each other's fears.*

*To change the outcome, Ms. Loner tried
something different. When people came to her
confronting her with Mr. Leader's negative
comments, she turned the conversation around.
Instead of justifying herself to the other person,*

she asked that person what they thought about what he said. She also guided the conversation toward ways Mr. Leader's ideas and hers could work together. She encouraged the person to see both sides; thereby, taking the focus off herself and placing it where it belongs: on the common good.

This method was effective in helping her deal with the negative energy coming from Mr. Leader without putting herself in a proving or justifying position. It didn't, however, stop the energy. It allowed her to defuse it, but not stop it.

She remembered from experience that confrontation hadn't worked for her before. Thinking about it, she went to the boss with a fair approach.

First, she asked her boss to keep her concerns confidential. Second, she chose her words wisely. She said she wanted to make a formal complaint about her co-worker, Mr. Leader. She continued by saying that she believed he was as talented as she, but that their approaches were different and they disagreed on several things. Third, she shared how she was diffusing the negative gossip and then she made a request. She requested her boss observe Mr. Leader without confronting him for a few months and form his own opinion.

Her boss agreed to keep the information to himself and pay more attention to the work environment.

Ms. Loner did all she could and she let go of the outcome. In the meantime, she focused on standing in her own truth and keeping her responses to the negative energy as neutral as possible. To help bring her comfort with the situation, she turned to her friends for support and venting. She chose non-coworker friends so that she didn't repeat old behavior.

Gradually, over time, her boss received more complaints about Mr. Leader. He eventually confronted Mr. Leader about his negative behavior and gave him a warning. Mr. Leader became more negative. His focus started including other people rather than Ms. Loner.

Note here, because Ms. Loner didn't feed the gossip by defending herself, her connection to Mr. Leader weakened. His energy started being drawn to other people who would mirror the same vibration to him by playing the enemy's role.

Unfortunately for Mr. Leader, his boss eventually fired him. For Mr. Leader, this was very difficult, but it gave him the opportunity to be more honest with himself and heal his fears.

Ms. Loner healed her fear by changing her responses and accepting her life's purpose. She realized that if she wasn't meant to be a leader, the universe wouldn't continue to place her in leadership positions. As time passed, she found peace with herself and she was no longer swayed by someone else's opinion of her.

We can see in the above example that sometimes a more passive approach is the best way to handle conflict. Both Mr. Leader and Ms. Loner were accurate and skillful, so in that way, they both were right. This situation was more about personality clashes than who was the most productive.

A situation like this can manifest between two people in almost any situation. If we don't have a boss to intervene, then what do we do? We can do what Ms. Loner did; we diffuse the energy as much as possible and if necessary, have a heart-to-heart with the person involved. If that doesn't work, we may need to change and move on. If it is a family member and we can't write them off, then we may need to create boundaries and limit our time with them.

The most important lesson to learn in a situation such as this is to remember that we don't need to prove ourselves to anyone, ever. We do not have to justify our lives to the people around us. It's our life to live. Everyone gets one.

As long as there are different value systems, and as long as we disrespect and undervalue those differences, there will be a struggle. If we can embrace each other and our life path, we can see the value in those differences and be grateful for them. Without differences and diversity, we wouldn't learn new things about ourselves and grow. Acceptance, respect, kindness, and wisdom are the cornerstones of a happy life and a happy world.

We can evolve to a place without conflict and be in Bodhisaville. It is also true that there are many of us who need more hands on experience to understand our own creations. To tell the mind and heart to surrender and let go of wanting to attain something; to just be at peace, with self is a tall order. As long as we have lessons to learn and issues to heal, the universe confronts us with those insecurities. The trick is to keep on healing more and more and gradually get to a place that allows us to handle our fears wisely. This will eventually transform our fear completely. The old saying goes, "Master yourself and you become fearless."

Most of the time, struggle is created when we resist healing or change. In that way, it acts as a guide by keeping us on the right track. The struggle encourages us to question our behavior and choices when otherwise we wouldn't pay attention.

There is only one more thing to say about fear and struggle. Some of us assume that fear means survival fear, and though that is an aspect of fear, it isn't the one we repress. Some of us would also say we don't fear being hurt emotionally; that we can get over it and so on. Some of us believe we are courageous in our relationships and that we take risks and so on. It is indeed courageous to love, but our biggest, greatest fear isn't love. Our greatest fear is loving completely.

To love completely is to have a true union with another person. It doesn't mean merging; it means having both feet in the relationship without holding a piece of yourself back for protection. Half opened hearts don't apply. To love is to trust. You trust someone with the holiness of your heart and you trust yourself enough to give it.

Failed relationships are a known fear and very manageable. We have a tendency to create divorce. We draw people to us who mirror and match our negative patterns; therefore, we set ourselves up for failure. We attract our negative equal as well as our potential. It is possible to create a complete love in a current relationship that was created from old patterns, if both people change.

A single person would want to heal and be willing to do what it takes to attract an equal, loving, person to his or her self. Quality attracts quality and fear attracts failure. If we fail in our relationships, then we are attracting the wrong people based on the energy we are sending out. A single person would need to address their co-dependent, fear-based patterns in relationships and change his or her attitudes along with beliefs about these issues. It is the only way to attract a different kind of person who is capable of a healthy love.

Fear of being truly loved by someone and being that open, that honest, and that intimate is our greatest fear. We fear what it would mean and how it would feel. For most of us, that kind of deep love is an unknown fear, but even that isn't the reason we fear it. We fear it greatly because we know that if we create it, life's changes will take it away from us and we fear that its loss would be too unbearable.

It is this one fear at our core that creates the negative relationship patterns we have with our loved ones. We fear the openness of it. We worry it will take us over; that to open fully would mean we would have to give something up. *If we have to give up a piece of ourselves, then it isn't love.*

We also fear the pain. Even if we succeed at a true love, death will take one person away from the other and there will be great pain. The love shared will go on, but so will the missing.

We all know that love lives forever and most of us believe we will be reunited with our loved ones when we pass away from this life. This belief brings us comfort; it doesn't provide an escape, however. It doesn't save us from the process of the pain.

The fear of the pain can cause us to partially close our hearts. This is especially true if we have lost a close family relative. Love can feel too painful and a complete adult love with a lover can be too devastating if lost.

To help us work with this energy, we need to decide to want a complete love anyway despite the fear, and live in the moment. This might represent great pain to some, but the joys make it worthwhile. Pain can be temporary, but joy is eternal. The alternative is to be alone for eternity, which is unlikely.

"ABUNDANCE ATTRACTS ABUNDANCE."

Parable Twelve
Journal Entry

"Divine Destiny"

I close my eyes and I breathe deeply. I let my mind go and I fly to the Angels. For a while, I float from one color to another and eventually I settle on the bench beside the river.

Looking around, I realize it has changed. I see a wooden bridge that goes over the river to

the left of the bench. Across the river I see
golden light. Turning around, I see a forest and
a circle of Angels.

I stand up and walk around the bench. Ryan
steps out from the circle of Angels and gives me a
warm hug. "We have gifts for you, Seeker."

He waves his hand, and the bench turns around,
facing the circle of Angels with the river at its back.
"Sit. You will enjoy this. This is your Angelic
council. They each share special gifts and guidance
that help you along your path."

I wasn't sure how to respond, so I bowed my
head slightly and sat down on the bench. Ryan
moves to my side as another Angel brings me a
large white, ceramic bowl of energy. "This is love
and healing. Anytime you are in need, partake of
the energy." Setting the bowl down, the Angel steps
back and joins the circle.

The next Angel steps forward and is holding a
golden crown. She places the crown on my head

and I feel energy flow from the crown all the way to my feet. "This crown represents your growth into higher consciousness. Congratulations."

Several more Angels bring me gifts, setting them at my feet. I can feel this overwhelming love and I begin to cry.

Then I see one Angel pushing a white cart. On this white cart is a stack of gold books that glitter with brilliance. He takes one of the golden books with a purple marker about halfway through and puts it on my lap. I hug the book to my chest and I can feel before he even tells me the energy of the book. Tears are rolling down my face. I close my eyes and keep hugging the book.

The Angel touches my hand. "The purple marker represents your placement." I look at the marker and see that it is about halfway through the book. I look at the cart and see that there are several more books to process yet.

"The books represent spiritual wisdom that is now available to you, Seeker. You have transformed enough fear and illusion that these books are attainable for you." He pauses a moment and says, "These gifts, including these books, have always been here for you. You have just finally allowed yourself to see and receive them. Your mental and emotional vibration has evolved enough to be compatible with the vibration of these gifts. Congratulations, Seeker, you are on your way to a better life!"

The Angel steps back and joins the others. I feel joy and relief. The relief is there because sometimes I thought I was losing my mind and at other times I thought I was going backwards. It is a relief to know that I made progress, that my progress isn't determined by complete understanding, but by my intention and commitment to heal.

All the Angels fade into the light away from my sight except Ryan, who sits down on the bench beside me. He extends his arm and gestures towards the gifts. *"These gifts and the abundance they represent have always been here. Spirit was waiting for you to feel worthy enough to receive them."*

I look down at the golden book in my lap and smile. *"I have so much more to learn,"* I sigh.

"We would rather you think that you have so much more to receive; that the next level of your path is more joyful and peaceful."

"How did this happen?"

"Do not allow your doubt to take this away from you, Seeker. You are ready to take your life to the next level. That bridge over the river is your doorway."

"Are you saying, Ryan, that I need to walk over that bridge to the other side?"

"Yes."

"I am afraid to move forward. It feels like once I cross over that bridge, I will have more spiritual responsibility."

"Seeker, you can't undo your spiritual awareness and in that way, there is no going backwards once you know better. It is more painful for you to sit here in between your old fear and your new joy. Dreams require doing."

"I don't know how to be happy. I don't know how to be abundant, not at the levels this new path represents. What if I cross over that bridge and my life doesn't change? Does that mean I have failed?"

"Again I will say, Seeker, do not let your doubt take this away from you. It is you, and you alone, who judges your success and failure. To us, the Angels, it is impossible for you to fail. You are already a success because you have made the choice."

"What choice?"

"You have made the choice to heal and to love. You have made the choice to transform your fear back into love. You have made the choice to live consciously and with integrity. You have made the choice to stand in your power and release victimhood energy. You have made the choice to be who you really are; a Divine being. Therefore, you cannot fail, since success is already a given." He smiles.

"Humans are only asked to do one thing: love to the best of their ability. Their ability to love is based upon the healing and transformation of fear. The less fear they have, the more they are capable of love and wisdom."

"Anything, including struggle, that helps you transform fear is in divine perfection. You don't have to worry about whether you will get to the end of your path. Your only concern is 'how' you want to get there."

"So get up, Seeker, and walk over that bridge!"

"What about all of these gifts?"

"They go with you, of course. Now stop stalling and get up."

"Will you come with me?"

"Of course."

I stand up with Ryan at my side and I walk to the bridge. As I look across the river, I can see a golden white path with two rows of trees on either side. They form a beautiful canopy over the path.

I step onto the bridge and walk to the other side. Ryan is with me, and I look around. I see that the gifts automatically traveled with me as they instantly appear around me.

Ryan touches my shoulder; "The gifts were here before you saw them and will be here always. They are limitless and eternal because they are an *extension of your own Divinity. You can use them repeatedly and never run out, because your Divinity is a piece of Goddess/God and it can never be drained. They represent your ability to love."*

*I nod my head in understanding and ask, "Where does this path lead?" "**To your Divine Destiny,**" he whispers in my ear.*

Chapter Twelve

"I am that I am Goddess/God"

"I am that I am" is said to be one of the most powerful affirmation a person can say. Notice that it is genderless and singular. Most of us expect this, I'm sure. What isn't looked at too often is the "I." We refer to ourselves with "I" and yet, we ignore the power of it.

We spend so much of our time hiding and protecting the "I" that we drain our energy, and it is the one thing that can set us free. We forget that the "I" doesn't need protecting, it just is. It needs no explanation or justification.

We spend too much time dwelling on insecurities, deciding if we are good or if we are bad, and so on that we get lost in the world of division. We are neither good nor bad. We are "I."

Life doesn't guarantee that only those of us who are good get to be without struggle. Life doesn't determine a difference between good or bad. Energy is energy, and when we stop judging it and see it for what it is, we can set ourselves free. Life is life. Accept it and live it by accepting both energies.

We cannot save a person from himself or herself, just as we can't save groups from themselves. We have the power to free ourselves and try to demonstrate kindness and wisdom in the best way we can.

This is our individual Divine Destiny. Some believe that walking a spiritual path is about peace, light, love, and all things good. Our spiritual paths are both positive and negative. We can be the wisest, most enlightened person on the planet, and yet we still live here in this reality. Everyday occurrences, like someone being rude to us, will still feel unpleasant and could create an emotional response or a natural disaster could destroy our home.

Humans are engineered to have emotional responses. They have purpose and are divine because of that purpose. So what do we do with them? We accept and we stop fearing them and placing judgment on them. We practice emotional honesty, and change our communication and relationship patterns by expressing our feelings in healthy ways. As we become more aware of our issues, we can work with them, continuing to walk down our spiritual path. This healing process allows us to focus on using our gifts and fulfilling our purpose.

We can be abundant with our gifts. Being abundant attracts abundance and sharing our gifts is effortless.

"I use and share what has been given, and in the sharing, abundance flows."

Our gifts come naturally to us and, therefore, they are the easiest things for us to share. If we feel stuck and tired, the best thing we can do is say, "Yes" when we have the opportunity to share our gifts. Some people fear that if they give when they are tired, it will lower the quality of their life. It is that fear-based attitude that creates stinginess. Everyone has natural born gifts and truly they are effortless to share with others. Long-term, sharing gifts with kindness will increase energy levels. The fulfillment and joy one feels nourishes the spirit and the body as long as a person doesn't give at the expense of his or her well-being. Giving time and energy to self is just as important. Our life-force energy needs to flow by receiving and giving to create abundance.

Our abundance is determined by our energy levels. It is the universal law of cause and effect. The universe matches or mirrors our energy at all times. If we are tired, things will usually slow down for us. If we don't use our talents in this life, we'll experience hardship and difficulty as a result. Happiness and success are created by using and sharing our gifts.

When we are down and out, we need to start somewhere. The best place to start is by giving. We have to start somewhere and by giving abundantly, in alignment with our gifts and on our own terms, and we will increase the flow of energy creating abundance. If we shut down because of resentment or victimhood, then we close the door of universal abundance.

The best place to start is with (time). Everyone can give time, and we won't resent it if we give it on our own terms. How do we do that? If we are a good listener, then we listen. If we don't want to give more than an hour to the other person, then we make an agreement with ourselves to kindly end the conversation and move on.

If we are a terrible listener and prefer action, then we can offer an invitation to do something.

Again, we would want to put a time limit on it and so on.

We also could help a friend in need, even if it is something as small as sending them a card or lighting a candle and saying a prayer for them. When we give, it doesn't have to be something big. It only requires that we open our hearts and when we open our hearts, our life is automatically more joyful.

Money is another area of energy. How do you increase your financial abundance when you are broke?
We have heard the mantra: pay yourself first, even if it's a dollar. However, we can go to financial advisors for that kind of information. Our focus here is emotional.

To increase our financial abundance, be conscious of our state of mind. Surrounding ourselves with one or two things that represent abundance helps keep our state of mind positive. For example, soft towels, sunset walks, ice cream cones; the list goes on and on. We have to be the energy vibration we want to attract to us.

(Close your eyes briefly and think about what represents abundance to you and see what symbols form in your mind. For some people, it's wood furniture, for example. Once you have a few symbols to work with, find ways to put them into your home. If the color red is one of your symbols, then use that color. If it's wood furniture, hit the garage sales and so on.)

Giving of ourselves, sharing what we have and what we are good at brings opportunities for more money. The key is to take action and do more than just think about it.

Let go of miser energy, especially on the small stuff. There is an old saying, "Penny Smart and Pound Stupid." Instead, we need to look at its emotional value. For example, when we are hosting an enormous event, if we scrimp on the food, people will be disappointed. Good food creates a pleasurable and generous experience. People attending the event will feel cared for and valued.

Let's say that we are in a hard spot that will take some time to change. We always have the power of choice to be kind, to be positive, and to trust. When we listen to our inner voice, it will guide us. Again, we are never alone. Our Angels are with us always. If we ask for help, they will help us provide for our families and ourselves. We need to show up and take action. Leave the details to Spirit.

When our energy is plentiful, it replenishes us. When we have everything we need, we have the motivation to give, even when it is hard.

It is said that using the "I am that I am" with intention statements is one of the most powerful tools we have at our disposal for manifestation.

Life may be hard, but it is always for our growth. If we surrender our judgments and stop trying to control it, we learn we are protected, loved, and sustained by the Divine life-force energy that created us. We always have been, no matter what life throws at us. It's a fact, it's a truth, live it, count on it!

I am that I am Divine.

I am that I am Compassion.

I let go of the need to protect myself through the ego.

I embrace and trust my Divinity, my Angels, and Goddess/God to protect me.

I am
I accept
I am abundant in all ways.

I am that I am Love.

Amen.

HEALING PRAYERS

In the following pages are healing prayers to help move your energy in positive directions during times of struggle. Healing prayers are more powerful if used, in conjunction with candles and altars.

Setting up a spiritual altar is a useful self-help tool that everyone can do regardless of background.

To set up an altar, you need a representation of the four elements, a representation of yourself, and a representation of Spirit.

Earth: rocks, crystals, herbs, flower, plants, sea salt, etc.

Air: feathers, flute, wind chimes, incense, etc.

Fire: hot herbs such as pepper, candles, symbols of the sun, etc.

Water: Seashells, bowl of water, picture of the moon, turtle, etc.

Spirit: cross, statues of angels, fairies, goddesses, etc.

You: a picture, favorite item or jewelry, etc.

To set up an altar, you can use a cloth, tabletop, TV tray, or any flat surface. The location should be private and quiet. Lay out the symbol for Earth in the North position of your altar, the symbol for Air in the East, the symbol for Fire in South, and the symbol for Water in the West. You put the items that represent Spirit and yourself in the center, along with a pillar candle.

The center pillar candle also needs to be prepared so that when it burns, it sends energy to your intention. With a pencil, carve your name and a prayer statement into the candle. Hold the candle to your heart, say the prayer three times, and ask Spirit to empower the candle to increase the energy. The color of the candle can influence the energy, but when in doubt, use white.

After you have set up your altar with the four elements, representation of Spirit and yourself, you can place the empowered candle in the center and light it. Light the candle each day until you have a resolution. When you want to extinguish the flame, use a candle snuffer; never blow out a candle unless you are completely done with it. If your candle runs out before you have resolution, then empower another and place it on the altar.

Another step to add, but optional, is to write down your prayer on a piece of paper and then burn the paper in a burning bowl. As the paper burns, the prayer travels from the Earth plane to the Spiritual plane flowing up to Goddess/God.

Candle color suggestion: purple, blue, white or black

Healing Prayer for Pain

As the wind blows,
Fire burns
The Earth stirs
And water flows

Working together in harmony,
Healing takes place.
All anger and pain are erased.

In the name of Goddess/God
So mote it be
Amen

Healing Prayer of Peace

May I stay centered
Filled with light and love.

With Goddess/God's
embrace
And Angel's grace.

Be still my heart,
Clear my mind,

May all fear be erased.

In the name of Goddess/God
So mote it be
Amen

Candle color suggestion: white, yellow,
green or blue

Healing Prayer for Confidence

May I be confident
And as bright as the sun.
To speak my truth
With clarity
As I manifest my reality.
In the name of Goddess/God
So mote it be
Amen

Candle color suggestion: yellow, blue, or
white

Healing Prayer for
Manifestation
Earth of love,
Earth of power,
Help me now,
In this hour.

Blessed thee,
Blessed me,
Help me manifest my need.

Power of creation,
Miracle of Life,
Bring forth thy light.

So mote it be
As it should
In alignment with
My highest good.
Amen

Candle color suggestion: green, orange, black or white.

Healing Prayer for Relationships

Together, we joyfully walk forward, embracing a deeper understanding of love with compassion, trust, and faith.

Nurturing and renewing our emotional, mental, spiritual, and sexual connection.

Infusing the light of love in all areas of our relationship.

Coming together as two, living a life as one in harmony.

We are blessed times three
So mote it be

Amen

Candle color suggestion: red, pink, orange, green or white.

Healing Prayer for Wisdom

I activate my Divinity,
As I open to receive guidance,
From the Holy Trinity.

I call to the Angels,
Hear my prayer
Please come to me.
I will listen and before a days end,
May I see what you have sent to me.

Blessed thee,
Blessed me,
Times three.

In the name of Goddess/God
So mote it be
Amen

Candle color suggestion: white, yellow, or
purple.

*The previous prayers are generalized
and are a good place to start. Prayer
used with altars and a small ceremony is
a powerful way to help ourselves and ask
for help from the Divine. What we say we
are, we become.*